WINNING
WITH
DECEPTION
AND BLUFF

Also by the author.

Cyclopedia of Trial Practice. An eight-volume
    text found in law libraries and universities
    throughout the nation.
Trial Manual for Negligence Actions (1933)
Preparation Manual for Accident Cases (1935)
Editor of *Lawyers Medical Journal,* a quarterly

Sydney C. Schweitzer

WINNING WITH DECEPTION AND BLUFF

PRENTICE-HALL, INC., *Englewood Cliffs, N.J.*

Winning with Deception and Bluff
by Sydney C. Schweitzer
Copyright © 1979 by Sydney C. Schweitzer
All rights reserved. No part of this book may be
reproduced in any form or by any means, except
for the inclusion of brief quotations in a review.
without permission in writing from the publisher.
Printed in the United States of America
Prentice-Hall International, Inc., London
Prentice-Hall of Australia, Pty. Ltd., Sydney
Prentice-Hall of Canada, Ltd., Toronto
Prentice-Hall of India Private Ltd., New Delhi
Prentice-Hall of Japan, Inc., Tokyo
Prentice-Hall of Southeast Asia Pte. Ltd., Singapore
Whitehall Books Limited, Wellington, New Zealand
10 9 8 7 6 5 4 3 2 1

Library of Congress Cataloging in Publication Data
Schweitzer, Sydney Charles,
    Winning with deception and bluff.
    Bibliography: p.
    1. Success. 2. Persuasion (Psychology)
3. Deception. I. Title.
BF637.S8S38   158'.1   78-25798
ISBN 0-13-961268-8

Acknowledgments

The author's debts in writing this book are many and varied. A complete list of all those to whom I am indebted would no doubt impress the reader and put an undeserved halo of authority over what I have written, but it would be tedious. I cannot, however, fail to express my appreciation to Irene Graham and Susan Lubonne for their help in the preparation of the manuscript, and to Edna Boschen and Dennis Fawcett of the Prentice-Hall editorial staff for their assistance.

I also gratefully acknowledge permission to quote from the following copyrighted material:

The Figure Finaglers by Robert Reichard; *The Human Zoo* by Desmond Morris, *Inside Intuition* by Flora Davis; copyright by McGraw-Hill Co.

King of the Courtroom by Michael Dorman, copyright © 1969 by Michael Dorman and Dell Publishing Co; rights controlled by McIntosh and Otis, Inc.

1876—A Novel by Gore Vidal, copyright by Random House, Inc.

Illusion in Nature and Art; Yankee Lawyer, The Autobiography of Ephraim Tutt; copyright by Charles Scribner's Sons.

Power, Inc., by Morton Mintz and Jerry S. Cohen, copyright by Viking Press.

Heroes and Heroines of Fiction, by William Walsh, copyright by Lippincott Company.

Excerpt from editorial in *News-Sun,* Sun City, Arizona, copyright News Sun Company.

My Life in Court by Louis Nizer; copyright 1961 by Doubleday & Company Inc. Excerpt from editorial in *New York Times,* copyright, The New York Times Company.

Contents

What This Book Is All About *ix*

Foreword *xi*

1. **The Statistical Trap** *1*
2. **The Great Put-On** *23*
3. **The Executive Masquerade** *37*
4. **Lawyer Put-Ons** *77*
5. **The Research Project** *85*
6. **The Diversionary Ploy** *93*
7. **One-Upmanship, Forget It** *109*
8. **Who—Not What** *117*
9. **Stroke Him, Man, Stroke Him** *127*
10. **The Manipulated Response** *139*
11. **That Beautiful Man of Straw** *147*
12. **The Illusion of Relevancy** *155*
13. **The Weight of Ethos** *167*
14. **Word-Fog, Half Truths, No Truths, and Miscellaneous Deceptions** *175*

Notes *185*

What This Book Is All About

I made a disconcerting discovery during my first year in practice as a lawyer in New York City. The woods were full of poseurs—mediocrity and crass incompetence posing as ability, not only in the profession itself but in the judiciary. To a starry-eyed young lawyer, this was upsetting. When I talked it over with an old-timer at the bar, a shrewd observer of the scene, he remarked: "You'll grow up and get used to it. Every profession, every business, has its share of put-ons."

The message lingered. You needed a put-on, something to lift you out of the common mass, to give you winning credentials, even if you didn't deserve them.

So less than a year after graduating from St. John's University, School of Law (in the middle of the Great Depression), I began to write a law text on how to try a case in court, a subject of perennial interest to lawyers. I had yet to try my first case. The book was accepted by a law publisher, even before its completion. I was told it needed an imprimatur. So I submitted the manuscript to Judge Frederick Evan Crane of the New York Court of Appeals, the state's highest court.

He was over-charitable, may God bless his soul, when he wrote a preface, describing my book as a great contribution to the legal profession. The text, a hefty volume of 1,000 pages, went through seven printings and three editions, and has since grown to an encyclopedia of eight volumes, found in law schools and law libraries throughout the nation. It was, for many years, the best-selling work on trial strategy. I have used it myself repeatedly in the years of trial work that followed its publication.

This start was, I must admit, a put-on, much like an intern, never more than an observer in the operating room, writing a book for the medical profession on how to perform a laminectomy.

Now, forty-five years later, I have come to a few conclusions about the human scene generally. Simply stated:

1. Deception and bluff increasingly rule the roost in human affairs.

2. Manipulative deceits, sharpened by lawyers, statesmen, politicians, and business leaders, hide behind growing mounds of high-sounding garbage.
3. With a little practice, you Mr. or Ms. Average Person can learn to tap this arsenal of Machiavellian maneuvers.

My purpose is not merely to describe these deceits. Exposé books glut the market. Nor am I sounding a call to arms against the manipulators. This would be an exercise in futility. My purpose is more practical, you will discover, as you get into the book.

This work was not, believe me, written tongue-in-cheek. The title will no doubt offend or amuse you, and frankly, it was intended to do both. Titles sell books. I have used most of the maneuvers described, and I ask you to do likewise, adapting them to your own talents and inclinations.

Foreword

Let us concede at the outset that we live in a world full of persuaders—and that not all of them are ethical. And let me offer as a further proposition—and as a partial justification for this book, and its outrageous title—that a working knowledge of Machiavellian behavior can be not only a helpful and entirely legitimate aid in your everyday activities, but a countermeasure to aggressive behavior by others, a rational defense against manipulation or intimidation, in whatever form.

Cornell University's Graduate School of Business Administration once conducted a seminar on "extra-legitimate" behavior, using as its text Machiavelli's sixteenth century handbook *The Prince*.

The course was reported to have stirred considerable controversy, including suggestions that Cornell might also offer courses on Jack the Ripper, Attila the Hun, the Borgia clan, and the Marquis de Sade. The instructor, who received his own Machiavellian training in the advertising business, cautioned his princelings that the motivation is merely rational, dispassionate self-interest. In approving the course the Dean argued that the world is "not a just and kindly place and never will be, and I'm not interested in sending our students out of here as sheep to be shorn."

Machiavelli put it realistically when he said:

> . . . for how we live is so far removed from how we ought to live, that he who abandons what is done, will rather learn to bring about his own ruin than his preservation. A man who wishes to make a profession of goodness in everything must necessarily come to grief among so many who are not so good. Therefore it is necessary for a prince, who wishes to maintain himself, to learn how not to be good, and to use the knowledge and not use it, according to the necessity of the case.
>
> —————— *Machiavelli, The Prince, p. 84*

Effective persuasion, or, to put it more bluntly, deception in one form or another, is more than verbal duelling or cleverly turned phrases, more than just relating to your listener. And more than "just being truthful, with hard facts as your ammunition." A schoolboy knows that facts rarely persuade. The truth is too often unpalatable. The French painter Fougeron vividly depicted this in his starkly realistic work "The Naked Truth," showing a crowd turning aside and fleeing from, rather than facing, the ultimate reality of truth.

To put it differently, belief is rarely the result of reason. It needs an infusion of deception. We believe what arouses our desires and stirs the emotions. Thinking is not a painless process. To escape its strictures, we invent a myriad of delusions. "My attitude is conviction. Yours is prejudice."

Yet I believe with Matthew Arnold that while we do not always change our minds as a result of logic or reason, under proper persuasion the ground slowly shifts beneath us, the view changes ever so slightly, and we find that things no longer look the same. *But what makes effective persuasion?* Why do some attempts die stillborn, while others make such ground swells in changing opinions or creating desires? The difference, simply stated, lies in mastery of the art of deception and bluff. The lures tempt you on all sides, at all levels: in your office, your business, the courtroom, newspaper ads, magazines, radios in the home and car, television; when you open your mail or a pack of matches, or watch the billboards as you drive your car—they are there in one form or another.

Winning With Deception and Bluff is not a primer on how to recognize knavery or how to cheat your fellowman. The maneuvers described are legitimate. They break no law. But they may help you to make out in a world that is not always kind to the honest and trusting.

Sydney C. Schweitzer

Dedicated to the hope that somewhere in the vast universe there exists a civilization whose inhabitants are unschooled in the arts of deception and bluff.

Good usually must follow a narrow path with few options open to it, while Evil is left free to do whatever it believes will win the day. Thus Evil is opportunistic, exploiting every opening, while Good is usually prevented from taking advantage of such opportunities.

———————————————————— *Machiavelli*

. . . this was the great, abiding lesson of my boyhood: that I was in a world where it was *not possible* for me to be good.

———————————————————— *George Orwell*

1. The Statistical Trap

Oh, that deceit should steal such gentle shapes and with a virtuous vizard hide foul guile![1]
——————————— *Lament of the Duchess of York*

The sheer number of quantitative distortions now seems to have reached the epidemic stage, threatening to mislead the innocent and instill an intense dislike for anything statistical or quantitative on the part of the more informed.[2]
——————————— *The Figure Finaglers*
Robert Reichard

Prelude to Deception

There was a time—and what a wonderful time it was—when percentage formulae, sampling techniques, and statistical manipulations were unknown. Now you can start with a single fact and juggle it to a variety of impressive conclusions, depending on what best suits your purpose.

You can, for example, describe a 1% return on sales as a ten-million-dollar profit, a 15% return on investment, an increase in profits of 40% (compared to the preceding four-year period), or a decrease of 60% from last year, and prove any one of them by statistical manipulation.[3]

You can easily sugarcoat the fact that your business lost money over a stated period. Simply follow the tactic of one company spokesman: "A statistical survey will disclose that while our profits showed a healthy increase for each quarter of the year, the gains were not sufficient to indicate a profit increase for the year."

There's little doubt that you can, after reading this chapter and with a little practice, juggle figures or draw charts, graphs, or diagrams to prove the legitimacy of any statistic you offer. I once heard Stuart Chase remark that Americans like ice cream and statistics because they slip down so easily. The more graphs and illustrations accompany the figures, the easier they go down.

There's a finality and halo of authority about statistics that too often discourages questioning and analysis. Where you feel that the figures offered are basically unfair to a posture you are trying to establish, don't despair. Try a different yardstick. Wondrous indeed are the gymnastics you can perform with numbers.

> There are lies, damned lies, and statistics.
> ——————————————————— *Mark Twain*

Oral Roberts, the popular evangelist, notes that ancient Hebraic folklore invests the number "seven" with a mystical wholeness, a promise of fulfillment, and he points to his own last name as a seven-letter word. There is a curious magic to numbers, a heady brew of persuasion and deception. An ancient seer claimed that numbers rule the universe, and sought to prove his point by endowing numerals with moral qualities:

One for reason, two for opinion, four for justice, five for marriage—the last being formed from the union of the first male number, three, with the first even, or female, number, two. Some eight hundred years later St. Augustine explained that if "God created all things in six days it was because this number is perfect"—its divisors, one, two, and three, totalled itself.[4]

Mark Twain pointed out the power of statistics in this gem from *Life on the Mississippi:* "In the space of 176 years the Lower Mississippi has shortened itself 242 miles. This is an average of a trifle over one mile and a third per year. Therefore, any calm person, who is not blind or idiotic, can see that in the Old Silurian Period, just a million years ago next November, the River was upward of 1,300,000 miles long, and stuck out over the Gulf of Mexico like a fishing rod. And by the same token, any person can see that 742 years from now the Lower Mississippi will be only a mile and three-quarters long, and Cairo and New Orleans will have joined their streets together. . . ."

To the modern entrepreneur, the manipulative ploys are only too well known; to the Average Person the world of statistics is a labyrinth beyond one's capacity to clearly analyze, much less use to one's own advantage in everyday activities.

This chapter may appear to be a manual on how to cheat and deceive. It can be justified with somewhat the reasoning of a retired stock manipulator or land fraud figure who writes a book on how to market a phony stock issue or sell swamp land as a retirement paradise. The deceivers know all the gimmicks; you, the honest reader, need them in self-defense.

I propose to offer a few manipulative stratagems.

Use Percentages Wherever You Can. They Have The Largest Manipulative Potential   Percentages have a responsibility all their own. "Six out of ten" conveys the message, but "60%" is more impressive, more authoritative, hinting of research and analytical study. Look around you and notice the important role that percentage manipulation plays in shaping the public pronouncements of corporations and creating the right corporate image.

Consider, for example, the report of a steel company that its employees' average weekly earnings went up 107% in a stated period. It neglected to mention that the first year's figure during that period included a large number of partially employed workers. Obviously if you work half time one year and full time the next, your earnings will double. That says nothing about the wage rate.

If you want to lessen the impact of percentages that you don't like, try burying them in explanatory text. They become less prominent and more confusing. For example: "Among the males that returned the questionnaire, 15.6% reported intercourse with their wives or lovers less than three times weekly; 22% more than three times, but less than five; 40% more than three times a week, but less than ten times," etc., etc.

> Never eat in a restaurant named "Mom's," never play poker with a man called "Doc," and never trust a percentage figure.

Percentages can so easily be made to speak with a forked tongue. For example, the government announced an increase of 10% in the average income of persons below the poverty level, while the average salary of corporate presidents rose only 3%. No big deal. The poor's average increase was $400; the corporate heads gained $3,000.

No less tricky was the oil industry attempt to water down rising complaints about its high profits. It reported that its earnings from petroleum operations during the past year amounted to only 2.5¢ per gallon of sales. What it did not report was the number of gallons sold or the increase in its net profits.

Try applying a solid percentage statistic to a related but dissimilar situation, if it will help what you're trying to prove. This tactic is sometimes difficult to execute and make plausible. Still, it's worth a try. Nothing works all the time, and so many things work most of the time. Consider a hypothetical example:

Labor Union Wins Small Concession

"The demands of the Wicker Workers Union for a $2.00-per-hour boost to $6.40 an hour were rejected; management's offer of $.40 per hour was finally accepted, giving the union only 20% of the original offer.

This contrasted with the previous year union victory in winning 80% of its demands for a pay raise from $4.00 to $4.50 an hour. The final pact called for $4.40 an hour. Obviously, the union was more moderate the second time around, agreeing to accept 80% of its demands the first year, but only 20% the second year."

Pure hocus-pocus. Read the figures carefully. What the union got was the same in both years; $.40 an hour.[5]

Avoid this stratagem where the relationship you seek to establish would be too transparent a deception; as for example in this editorial comment:

> An organization called the National Back to God Movement is lobbying for legislation which it hopes would legalize voluntary prayer in the nation's schools and other public institutions.
>
> To support its case, the organization offered statistics to show that forcible rape, robbery, aggravated assault, murder, crimes against property, and crimes of violence increased dramatically in the 1960–1970 decade. The charts are accompanied by a comment that in June 1962 and June 1963 the Supreme Court ruled against prayer in the schools.[6]
>
> ——————————————— *Sun City (Arizona) News*

Statistics also show that during the same period the Boston Red Sox did not win a pennant or even finish second.

Don't Weaken a Percentage By Disclosing Its Base. "A survey disclosed that 74% of those interviewed approved the record of our Mayor."

"Eighty-two percent of those questioned by a team of interviewers preferred our brand of cigarettes to *any* of its competitors."

How many were interviewed? Twenty or two hundred?

More important, how valid a cross-section was used? The *Literary Digest* poll in the Roosevelt-Landon contest of 1936 was a fiasco, because it was largely confined to lists of telephone users. The editors overlooked that telephones then were a luxury to a large segment of the population.

Disclosing the precise base for a percentage estimate would obviously make for more reliability. Hiding or shading it may or may not be dishonest, depending on your point of view, but it can in many cases help you make something credible.

"Research has demonstrated that 75% of those we interviewed got relief with Stomach Aid within two minutes."

True, but deceptive. Omitted is the fact that the test involved only 12 people, with 9 reporting relief. Test enough small groups, and sooner or later you'll come up with the percentage you want.

You could also hire an independent sampling organization—one with recognized credentials, beyond chicanery or deception. Order a survey of two consumer groups, one using your product and the other using two major competitive brands. If the results of the first survey are not to your liking, order another test. Sooner or later, by operation of chance, you'll strike pay dirt—a report you can hang your hat on, and use in an advertising campaign.

There is also room for chicanery in the way you announce the results of a survey. You just don't show both sides of the coin, if one side only will make your point.

For example, a polio vaccine was tested some years ago. Of 1,100 children, 450 were vaccinated, 650 left unvaccinated. An epidemic visited the community shortly thereafter. Not a single vaccinated child contracted polio. An impressive tribute to the vaccine? Hardly. The other side of the coin was no less impressive: not a single one of the unvaccinated got the disease.

Vagueness helps. Your statement can be so worded that it covers all bases, yet touches none. Take this innocuous gem: "A miracle soil nutrient. Increases plant growth 20%." 20% over what? What type plant? In what climate and what kind of soil? Your imagination supplies whatever answer your hopes suggest.[7]

There's a difference. A magician gives you illusion that looks like truth. I give you truth in the pleasant disguise of illusion.

I represented a young lady who, while using a rose spray in her garden, sustained skin damage when the powder blew over her exposed hands, arms, and shoulders, resulting in a disfiguring and permanent condition known as vitiligo. The manufacturer, in its defense, offered a test on volunteer subjects in a Texas prison, with not one reporting even minor skin irritations. Impressive, but phony. Questioning disclosed that the test embraced only eight subjects.

As valid as the estimate I read of the rodent population in a city, based on a survey of the rats in one neighborhood. What of the rats hiding in the woodwork or plumbing? Or those that were counted twice as they ran from one floor to another, or that simply fled the building as the investigators did their investigating?

I wondered how many readers of the report questioned a projection of the visible rodent count in a few buildings to the entire city. Yet when dressed up as a statistic this cockamamie figure became respectable, no less than the dog or cat counts for an entire city, or the number of fish in a lake, or the report that "forty million pounds of dog dung are deposited annually in the streets of New York."[8]

You conjure visions of fleets of garbage trucks with scales, scooping up the dog droppings scattered over the Big Apple, carefully weighing each scoopful, then calling in the result to a central station, where computer banks arrive at a grand total.

> The trouble with people is not that they don't know, but that they know so much that ain't so.
> —————————————————— *Josh Billings*

Not long ago, a northern Congressman bewailed the fact that in one county in Arkansas, 78% of the white population was registered, but not a single black. He failed to mention that only two blacks lived in the entire county.

I was particularly intrigued by a report in a New York newspaper warning that just a year ago, 117 teams of con artists descended on the city. Not 116 or 118, mind you. Just 117. Did they check them in at the border?[9]

It was reported long ago, when Johns Hopkins University began to admit women students, that one-third of the women married faculty members. Actually, there were only three women enrolled in the school, and one of them had married a member of the faculty. That's much like the advertisement of a corporation announcing that its stock was held by 3,000 persons, with an average of 660 shares each. What it failed to reveal was that, of the outstanding two million shares, three men hold three-quarters.[10]

Always look for possible use of that magic persuader "random sampling" in whatever you're trying to establish. It's a common ploy you encounter in all media. The joker is the word "random."

You want to show the high percentage of users of your product. So you ask a reputable sampling organization to interview at random shoppers in a supermarket where your product has a good track record, avoiding stores where you're lowest on the list.

Contrived? Unquestionably, but still a random sampling within the common usage of that term.

Never Trust Round Figures or Sweeping Generalities   You would like to emphasize the number of purchasers of your product. Follow the example of a skin creme manufacturer who advertised *"150,000 women can't be wrong."* Not true! A million women can be, and have been, wrong. Still, your statement would be legitimate puffery.

No less incredible is the statement of a psychiatrist that his experience supports the view that three out of four people are neurotic, in one form or another. No doubt he reached this edifying conclusion from studying his own patients. How many "normal" people consult a psychiatrist?

I read in an AAA publication distributed to its members that statistics show drivers are less prone to accidents during the night than the day. *Ergo:* It's safer driving at night. Not so. The basis for the estimate is omitted, namely that more people drive during the day, hence a higher incidence of accidents.

Consider this neat manipulation: Recent Government statistics show Pall Mall 100's lower in tar than the best-selling filter king. True. Pall Mall did have a tar rating a minuscule less than Winston, but it also had more tar than 45 other brands of cigarettes.

Deception? Perhaps not, but certainly no more than spitting distance from it.

A large insurance company widely advertises:

"$100 billion is a lot of protection. To millions of Americans, that astronomical figure becomes something very real, very close, very personal. It means peace of mind. A sense of security."

A clever manipulation of a mind-boggling figure. To translate the amount of outstanding insurance into a solid asset is deception. There could be $100 billion of policies written (actually a potential debt) but only a fraction of that in cash in the till to satisfy claims in event of a major catastrophe.

A narcotics agent recently boasted of his haul of $1 million worth of heroin. An impressive but manipulated figure, if you'll think about it for a moment. His estimate is based upon a host of variables: the wholly unpredictable street price after the drug has been diluted, the amount of dilution, at whose hands, and the net return after the drug has been wholesaled and distributed down a line of pushers, sellers, and protectors. The real worth of his haul may be no more than a tenth of the figure quoted.

The New York Police Department reported some years ago a 30% decrease in crimes of violence for the preceding year. True, and not true. Assaults and similar crimes did, in fact, drop off, but an investigative committee reported: "What the Police Commissioner is not telling the public is that there has been, in the past year, a murder increase of 40%, the highest increase in the city's history."[11]

The Kinsey report on the sexual acrobatics of our population is steeped in so many charts and diagrams that it carries the weight of a papal encyclical. But to a statistician the report is riddled with arithmetical errors. It wasn't clear, for example, how many men were actually studied. On one page it stated that 12,214 men were interviewed. Elsewhere a map showed 427 dots, each said to represent 50 men, making a total of 21,350 males. The age groupings showed similar variances.[12]

Even assuming the accuracy of the charts, common sense points out the fallacies in the conclusions. How many of the men interviewed honestly reported on their sexual preferences or prowess? How about the male ego that numbers ejaculations per night as badges of machismo power? Or the female reluctance to admit to the full range of women's sexual likes and dislikes?

A house-to-house survey was made to study magazine readership. All types of neighborhoods throughout the nation were used; rich, middle-class, poor. The carefully tabulated count, showing *Harper's* preferred over *True Story*, flatly contradicted the circulation figures. *Harper's* sold in the thousands, *True Story* in the millions. The survey uncovered no more than snobbery. A more accurate count would have been obtained if they went to the houses and simply asked to buy old magazines.[13]

You want to show the popularity of a household appliance your store is selling, one that is more expensive than competitive brands. Simple. Hire reputable pollsters to conduct a house-to-house survey, but only in the areas you designate—the more affluent neighborhoods, avoiding the low-income and middle-class areas. The results, honestly tabulated, are likely to give you a percentage you can advertise. This is almost like polling the audience at a KKK meeting on their preference for Governor: the white or black candidate.

> Ninety percent of the game of basketball is half mental.
> ————————————— *Comment by a basketball star.*

The approximations often border on the ridiculous, as in the case of the psychologist who reported in a TV interview that, in his opinion, 20% of the male population had homosexual experiences, or the head of a Gamblers Anonymous who stated that 15% of our population were anonymous gamblers who needed help. You wonder if these authorities have powers of divination not given to other mortals, or if possibly they found Orwell's Big All-Seeing Eye.

No less intriguing is the report of a London research biologist that a rise in England's birth rate began ten months after the government reduced the lead content in gasoline.[14]

To Make an Increase in Total Costs More Impressive, Add the Percentage Increases   Adding percentages can give you an impressive figure. Barbers claim the price of a haircut must be increased from $3.00 to $4.00, in line with the 33% increase in the cost of their operation. They cite impressive figures: electric bills up 12%, rent up 11%, material 10%. A total increase of 33%, which is misleading. If *each* of these items had risen 10%, the total increase in costs would be just that: 10%.

But tread carefully in juggling percentage decreases; for example: "Corn is a bumper crop this year, selling 100% cheaper than last year." Impossible, unless it is being given away free.

No less tricky: "The severe drought has reduced the corn crop to 110% less than last year's." Less than zero is still zero.

A manufacturer reports its production expenses have risen 15% over the past three years, material cost 10%, sales expense 20%. Combined boosts 45%. But look carefully. If, for example, *each* item rose 12%, the total increase must also have climbed by that figure. Not one decimal higher.

Go to a supermarket and buy twenty different brands of cereals. You find that each has risen 5% over the preceding year, thus adding up to a 100% increase. Your addition is correct, but your conclusion is obviously out in left field.

Project the Percentage of Change in the Cost of One Item Onto the Overall Costs of All the Items   A few years ago, New York City landlords sought a 15% increase in rents, citing a 10% rise in fuel costs and a 15% increase in the cost of janitorial services. They failed to mention that interest payments, their *single* biggest expense, had remained the same. A neat and not uncommon maneuver of landlords. New York City's Rent Stabilization Board, after a comprehensive study, found that the overall costs rose only 4% annually, which was the increase they finally approved.[15]

No less guilty of the same basic deception is the entrepreneur who justifies the need to raise his prices 7% because his labor costs have risen by that amount, omitting entirely the amount of increase (or decrease) in other items of expense.

Remember this ploy if you're a manufacturer or retailer seeking to justify raises in prices. Pick the *largest* single increase, usually labor costs, then project this figure to the overall operational expenses. You may just get away with it.

Try Translating Large Increases to Large Percentages   The effect of phrasing increases in percentages is startling, and you may succeed in making it credible.

"There is no reason for this increase in oil prices. The company's earnings last year were 1,000% more than the year before."

What you are saying is simply that they are 11 times greater. (Not 10, if you will take the trouble to figure it out.)[16]

Try the Over-Precise Ploy   Wherever you quote statistics or figures, strive for precision, the more precise the better. Precision confers authority, over-precision inspires confidence.

"The appliances we sell are built to last. Only 2.15% of the refrigerators sold within the past year required service calls."

You know instinctively they must have carefully tabulated the figures, or else how could they have come up with the exact percentage?

The *World Almanac* of 1950 reports there are 8,000,112 people in the world who speak Hungarian. The final 112 is intriguing. It will either impress you with the thoroughness of the research, or turn you off completely.

François Rabelais used over-precision with telling effect in describing one of Gargantua's feats: "Thereupon Gargantua climbed to the towers of the Cathedral of Notre Dame and drenched all the spectators with such a bitter deluge of urine that he drowned two hundred sixty thousand four hundred eighteen, not counting women and children. A certain number escaped this doughty pisser by lightness of foot."[17]

Fit the Figures to Your Target   Corporate executives like to fix targets for production, sales, profits, or employee turnover, and when they miss, ingenious games are played to soften or hide the miscalculation.

A company manager assures the board there will be, for the ensuing year, a 25% return on investment. When he misses the target, he simply concocts figures to put his estimate in a more realistic light. Prices slipped 5%, construction expenses rose 20%, labor costs increased 10% over the projected estimate. So, with a juggling of figures, the company can still report a 25% return on investment, hiding the discrepancies in charts and graphs, with extensive footnotes.

Corporations regularly survive misses of announced

targets, sometimes as wide as the Atlantic, without undue loss of prestige or stockholder confidence.

> Corporate integrity is a phrase that should be divorced on the grounds of incompatibility.

Vague Is Sometimes Better   Deception wears so many faces in statistical manipulation, it is often difficult to distinguish between the honest and dishonest. Vagueness is a ploy you can sometimes use to take the sting out of a statistic you don't like. For example:

An advertisement by a group of electric companies reported some years ago that "Today's electric power is available to more than three-quarters of U.S. farms." Read this statement carefully.

It blurs the fact that one-quarter of the nation's farms lacked electric power or access to it, a shocking figure by itself. "Available" is vague to the point of being deceptive. It doesn't mean that three-quarters of the farms actually use electric power. As for availability, how far from the power lines are the farms— two, ten, or forty miles?[18]

Whenever statistics don't help to make your point, consider the familiar ploy of vague comparisons. "More people are eating our cereal than ever before," or "More housewives use our brand than any other." The first example is, of course, meaningless in statistical terms. There could be no more than a 1% increase in sales over the previous year. The second implies a majority over any other single brand—which is not necessarily so—the opposition could be scattered over a dozen brands.

Learn the Art of Shading   You can follow the conventional rules and chart all the relevant facts and still leave the reader with a false impression—the one you want him to accept. Using color illustrations, chart distortions, overlays, and explanatory notes to highlight the aspects you want to stress, you can easily disguise the unpalatable.

It is easy to rationalize that no deception is involved. You have merely emphasized one part of the overall picture. If the reader fails to use the right perspective, the fault is his—not yours. It's much like the seller of a condominium or yacht, who lists the rock-bottom price, sugar-coating or avoiding the many extras, without which you can't even begin to use your purchase.

Pick the Lowest Base to Show the Highest Increase   Where the base is scattered over several figures, pick the lowest to establish the heftiest increase. A campaign statement by a politician running for re-election in an eastern state pointed out that "the minimum teacher's salary in the state was as low as $6,000 a year, four years ago; today, our teachers earn among them the highest salaries in the nation."

The "before" and "after" comparison is pure gimmickry, but not unusual in statistical comparisons. Actually, out of thousands of teachers in the state, no more than a small handful in a few rural schools earned $6,000. Hardly a basis for an honest comparison.

Suppose you want to point out the niggardly advances in your salary; select for purpose of comparison a previous year with a peak not much lower than the current year. If you are a police official anxious to report a dramatic drop in specific crimes since you took office, compare the current statistics with a previous year with a much higher crime incidence. Deceptive, but not actually dishonest.

Correlation to the Rescue   Look for helpful correlations, even if distant as the moon, provided they have a measure of plausibility. It may help sell your product or prove your point. For example:

A New York modeling school planted this gem in a corner of its brochure: "A course in personal improvement and modeling will not only give you an opportunity to increase your earnings, improve your personality, and meet interesting people, it will also increase your prospects of marriage. Out of three hundred and four students in our school last year, over thirty-four percent married within a year after graduation. This was almost double the rate of marriage among girls graduating a large eastern university in the same period of time."

Impressive at first glance, but the conclusion falls apart on closer examination. The girl who elects a modeling career is not necessarily the same type as the girl who attends college to earn a degree. Furthermore, "the unwarranted conclusion has for its basis the equally unwarranted assumption" that the girls married simply because they attended a modeling school.[19]

Percentage or Percentage Points? Make Your Selection It can make quite a difference whether you cite a percentage or percentage points. Use whichever better scores the point you are trying to make. Assume your profits rise from 4% on investment one year to 8% the following year. You can honestly claim a modest increase of four percentage points. With no less honesty, you can boast of a 100% increase.

Smaller Is Sometimes Better A simple and often helpful stratagem for manipulating statistics is breaking down the big numbers to small digits. An oil producer, anxious to justify higher prices, recently reported that it earned no more than 2.5 cents per gallon of sales. True. What it did not tell was *how many* gallons it sold that year, or how much larger its net profits were than the year before.

Small numbers can also be less frightening. Prior to the Truth in Lending Law that took effect in 1969, sellers could advertise carrying charges at 1½% a month; now the true interest must be stated on an annual basis, which would make it 18% a year.

Manufacturing Your Own Statistics The trick is to use only those components that favor the average you want, ignoring the others or masking them so that they appear irrelevant or unimportant.

An all-too-familiar example:

A corporation, anxious to attract additional capital, reports substantial profits for three consecutive years. The losses of some of its subsidiaries are hidden by accounting gimmickry. The net profits of the winners are accurately reported. Tabulate the profits and losses of *all* its satellites, and you arrive at an average as sweet as it is phony.

A Central American dictator, anxious to hide the growing poverty of his nation, recently boasted of its growing wealth, choosing the arithmetic mean to show average income. He knew that the pittance paid to 97% of the working population, living only slightly above starvation level, would be favorably offset by the large income of a handful of wealthy landowners.

Manipulators have a field day with averages. Suppose you want a good image for your small business, to offset a union demand for higher wages. You report an average salary of $14,083.

1 Owner-Manager	$ 60,000
1 Office Clerk	9,000
10 Machine Operators (at $10,000 each)	100,000
	$169,000

Stated mathematically, the average is $14,083. Stated honestly, it's a different story.

Now suppose you are a real estate developer and want to establish the desirability of a nearby area by showing the high income of its residents.

"The average income is $20,000," you state, quite honestly, citing a poll conducted by a civic organization. They took the arithmetic average, adding all the income and dividing by the number of families. The maneuver is tricky, but legitimate. Unfortunately, it took little account of the retirees and low-income families. A dozen families could have earned over $100,000, boosting the misleading average sky high.

A news magazine reported that the average teacher earns $14,244, "well below the national median income for a family of four." Misleading. The median income of a family of four is higher because the average family of four has more than one wage earner. Obviously a median family income is higher than that for individuals.

Shift the Base to Take Advantage of Declines and Advances   Assume you have a sales decline of 50% in your business, from one million to half a million units, followed by an increase of 50% in the number of units sold. They would appear to cancel out, but not so. This is an illusion created by many corporations in juggling annual reports on sales and profits.

Obviously, the increase is on a different basis from the decrease. The latter base is one million; the base for computing the increase in volume is half that amount. The sales bounce on this figure raises the units sold to only 750,000. A tricky maneuver, difficult to detect in the corporate report.[20]

Drop the "Don't Knows" You are running for public office and hire a public opinion sampling organization to canvass voter response to a proposition you favor. The results show 40% in support of your stand, 10% opposed, and 50% no opinion. By dropping the "don't knows," you can report that 80% are in favor of the cause you espouse, and only 20% opposed. A thoroughly deceptive maneuver, fortunately not used today by responsible opinion samplers. But there's nothing to prevent Mr. Candidate from hiring and instructing his own group of pollsters.[21]

Sugarcoat Damaging Figures by Showing Them in Relative Terms Using relative rather than absolute terms may help soften the impact of figures you don't particularly like for one reason or another, or possibly make your position more believable, depending on what you are trying to establish. It can be argued, for example, that those over 65 represent no more than 10% of our population. A handy figure if you're trying to minimize their impact on the economy, and their influence in shaping cultural levels. But the other side of the coin is no less impressive. Ten percent represents 22 million people, with over 70% of them voting regularly.

20% Off List Price—This Week Only The offer quoted above is really no big deal, but if you are in the retail business, it may lighten your inventory. "List Price" can be easily manipulated, so that even with the 20% off, the sale price is just about the same as the regular market price. "Discount off list" is an increasingly popular form of deception. Distributors and manufacturers join in the game by offering rigged lists to the retailer.

Equally deceptive are the stickers on new cars, showing "list" or "suggested" prices. A survey by the Federal Trade Commission of 6,500 new car sales disclosed that less than 2% of American-made cars moved at these rigged prices.

Draw a Scale   A scaled chart, drawn to mathematical accuracy, is beyond manipulation. Right?

Wrong. Two simple devices, in common use by a wide variety of persuaders, from business corporations to municipal bodies and political candidates, will show you how easily you can manipulate a scaled drawing.

A favorite ploy is failure to place numbers in proper perspective, much like a photographer zooming in on a favorite subject, while shading or cutting out scenes that detract from the desired image.

To illustrate: You are a manufacturer anxious to show graphically in your advertisements the sharp increase in public acceptance of your product. The chart you offer depicting sales pushing upward over a three-year period is indeed impressive.

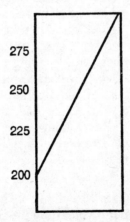

The deception lies in omission of the zero base. The bottom line is conveniently floated out of the picture. A more honest graph would use a base of zero sales, which obviously makes for a far less dramatic increase.

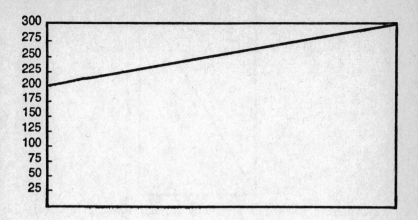

The news media have long used this ploy for greater impact on their readers. There is no question that using a floating or eliminated base makes for a more interesting chart.

A few statisticians, self-conscious about this duplicity—although many chartists refuse to admit any distortion—will draw a wavy and inconspicuous line at the bottom of the scale to indicate a base that has been floated upward. But it would require an unusually alert reader to notice the warning line (known as the zero break), much less understand what it meant, even with hieroglyphs accompanying it.

Which brings us to the second ploy, at which the Washington bureaucracy is particularly adept. This stratagem superimposes distortion of the scale dimensions on a graph already distorted by manipulation of the zero factor. Where, for example, a government agency seeks to dramatize the progress it made over a stated period, it will not only forget the zero line, but elongate the graph by narrowing its base. If, on the other hand, the bureau desires to minimize growth, as with inflation, it will simply flatten out the scale. To illustrate:

Assume consumer complaints rose from 10,000 to 12,000 in two years. You are a chartist employed by a governmental agency. Your chart will read thus:

Now suppose you are employed by the Manufacturer's Associa-
tion of America:

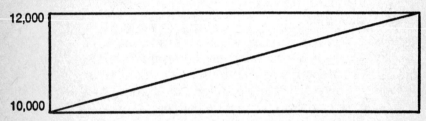

As one perceptive observer put it:
"The lesson is clear: Elongate the vertical scale, and the
amplitude of change is magnified; stretch out the horizontal
scale, and the magnitude of change is dampened."
To put it more simply, the same figures can show you
skyrocketing to new heights or just crawling along at pedestrian
pace.
So, if your attempt at deception or bluff occasionally demands proof of progress made, try a visual aid. A chart drawn to
scale is ideal for the purpose, provided it is drawn to *your* scale and
projected according to *your* dimensions.

Pictorial Charts   Easy to contrive and seemingly innocuous in
its simplicity, the pictorial chart is a common manipulative device.
Suppose you are a union organizer and want to emphasize your
claim that union wages in a certain industry are double those of
non-union workers in the same industry.

Impressive? But deceptive. The chart is more dramatic than any figures you could offer. The union worker stands twice as tall as the wages he receives. At least, that's what the pictograph suggests. But it suggests more, much more. The volumes of the space occupied speak of a far more hefty difference—something like a ten-to-one ratio.

This is a common ploy of statistical finaglers. It abounds in all media. You can adapt this device to almost any situation where figures would be too muted in their effect. The eye so easily confounds the mind!

Pick Your Frame of Reference   There is a beautiful simplicity to this maneuver. Suppose your candidate lost an election, receiving only 35% of the votes, while the winner got 45% and a third candidate 20%; or by count, 350,000, 450,000 and 200,000 votes respectively.

A decisive defeat for your man? Not quite. You can point out:

1. The winner did not receive a majority, only a plurality.
2. 55% of the voters rejected the winning candidate.

You have obviously softened the impact of the defeat. Now suppose you own a retail business. You decide to make up a financial statement. You can show earnings as follows:

1. A net profit of 1% of sales, no more than 1% on each dollar taken in, or
2. A 10% return on investment, or a $2,000,000 profit, or
3. 30% increase in profits over the past five years, or
4. 20% decrease in profits over the preceding year.

The first reflects the fact that the actual net profit is small, even with a hefty gross sales, after all the operating and other expenses are deducted. Could bankruptcy be around the corner with so razor thin a profit margin? Not quite. The second is also correct. You have invested at high interest rates the large volume of cash received in the course of business, thereby swelling your profit to two million.

Now suppose you want to resist union demands for a wage increase. Use the last category. It's as truthful as any of the others. You've simply picked the right frame of reference. And if you are reporting to stockholders, use the third set-out. It's no less honest.

2. The Great Put-On

Make-believe often assumes the nature of a magic ritual. Not only do people pretend to be what they are not, but by staging their pretense, they try to conjure up and bring to life a new aura of genuineness. "The strange thing is often this conjuring act succeeds, and we become what we pretend to be."[1]

———————————— *Eric Hoffer: The Passionate State of Mind*

Lying is universal—we *all* do it. Therefore the wise thing is for us diligently to train ourselves to lie thoughtfully, judiciously; to lie with a good object, and not an evil one; to lie for others' advantage, and not our own; to lie healingly, charitably, humanely, not cruelly, hurtfully, maliciously; to lie gracefully and graciously, not awkwardly and clumsily; to lie firmly, frankly, squarely, with head erect.[2]

———————————— *Mark Twain: The Decay of the Art of Lying*

Anatomy of a Put-On Traditional roles in business have changed, no less than the conflict situations that commonly arise between No. 1's and their subordinates, and between those in the same peer group. The new roles are unfamiliar and uncomfortable—put-ons are not a natural stance—but without a working familiarity with them, you are like a lamb in a field of wolves. And all the pronouncements of the business gurus about self-esteem, assertiveness, proper motivation, and positive thinking won't detract one cubit from your vulnerability in the human jungle—unless you add the one missing ingredient, which is what this book is all about.

"Your programming begins when you stick your head out of the womb, and what follows for the rest of your life is according to the script written by your parents before you were five. You won't change that *basic* you. Don't try."

From a lecture on how to make a million before you reach forty, by one who did.

This is, of course, pure garbage. Look around you. We live in a world of doctored images. We instinctively crave an image that pleases, draws admiration. To that end we put on a countless variety of pretensions, largely superficial and limited to what convention decrees is proper and fitting. Most of us are impaled under the glare of the Big Eye. A few—very few—have the courage to doctor the image, shaping it to winning form.

No phase of deception or bluff requires more polishing and planning than the put-on. Properly used, this maneuver can make you appear what you are not, and create an illusion of competency where none exists.

Every move we make is edged with a put-on of some sort, to build your ego, your credibility, the believability of what you're saying, or an error in what the other is saying. It can range from the minuscule to the blatant—but it's there, in the form of flattery, criticism, false humility, or naked puffery.

It used to be easy to tell the put-on from the real. Not anymore, with the increasing awareness of manipulative stratagems. Many of the most polished put-ons that burden company or government payrolls like useless dead weight don't look or sound different from you or me.

> I have always loved truth so passionately that I have often resorted to lying as a way of introducing it into minds that were ignorant of its charms.
>
> ———————————————————— *Machiavelli*

You don't have to be a genius to use the put-on to build a credible façade of competence. Mix a goodly dose of *chutzpah* with a fertile imagination and you have the basic ingredients for a first-class deception.

I had a client, a housewife in western New York, who dabbled in the stock market with more losers than winners. She decided to study for the not-too-difficult examination given by the New York Stock Exchange and qualify as a registered representative. She passed and immediately began advertising a weekly advisory service on market trends.

Her letter, glibly written, was no more than what she gleaned from Value Line, Babson's, Standard & Poor's, and other established services. But her business took off and became highly profitable. Her small office had all the accoutrements for a successful put-on: three telephones, a ticker tape, an uncluttered desk that reminded you of an executive above petty details, book shelves lined with weighty tomes like *The Sophisticated Investor* by Burton Crane, Graham and Dodd's *Security Analysis, The Psychology of the Stock Market,* etc.; line drawings, charts, and large graphs covered one wall, with a plaque that read: "The crowd never wins because the crowd is always wrong. And it's wrong because it always acts rationally." Charts on another wall showed decline-advance ratios, odd lotters' activity, and supply-demand correlations, with Greek-looking footnotes that I am sure were far beyond her comprehension.

"I can point to a dozen services no better or worse than mine. We're all big put-ons," she once remarked, giving me the title for this chapter. "My track record is not too impressive, unfortunately. But it's something like sex. Those who can, do; those who can't, write about it."

Her undoing came when she bought securities for clients, converting some of the proceeds to her own use. So, a promising career as a Wall Street prophet ended in a jail cell. Yet she was no more a poseur than many of the market prognosticators who wrap themselves in an aura of expertise.

> Modesty is hardly to be described as a virtue. It is a kind of
> fear of falling into disrepute.
> ───────────────────────────────── *Aristotle*

I heard a security analyst compare the progress of several stock
lists over a period of years, one selected by a random throwing of
a dart at a page of closing stock prices, the others compiled by
several topnotch advisory services and the trust departments of
large banks. You know the results.

Deception and bluff are born out of an infinite variety of
put-ons, but few as mystifying to me as the glut of market
prophets, as accurate as an astrologer's chart, yet successfully
peddling their predictions to a wide and sophisticated spectrum
of buyers.

A worldly and cynical Jesuit priest named Baltasar Gracian
wrote in the seventeenth century: "Very learned people are easy
to deceive because, although they are versed in abstruse matters,
they lack the more necessary knowledge of everyday affairs."[3]

> The profiles of an honest man and a successful business
> executive have become mutually exclusive.

I suspect that successful users of the put-on develop in time a
self-induced schizophrenia: one man in a black hat with
Machiavellian guile in his blood, adept at manipulating put-ons
and put-offs, a well camouflaged fox primed to spring at the
opportune moment; the other, in a white hat, weighted by moral
and ethical convictions, who holds his head high at the end of a
day's work, pride and conscience intact, oblivious to what tran-
spired before.

> You are not a liar unless you know you are a liar, for it is not
> a lie to speak an untruth in the belief it is true. Yet if a liar
> knows he is a liar and admits it, he must be a truthteller in
> denouncing himself as a liar.

Be realistic in the goal you set. Avoid the one-shot put-on that
brings you a one-shot success, but brands you forever after.

Balance the risks in your manipulative effort, whatever it may be, against possible benefits. The line between fraud and permissible deception is tenuous at best. Still, selling a gold brick is not the same as selling yourself or an idea to a prospective customer. You may redeem yourself with the latter, but you're dead with the former. You'll probably meet the other person again, and if you've deceived him with a sock-it-to-him or now-you-see-it/now-you-don't tactic, your credibility is zilch.

The manipulations described in this book will not assure success in every deceptive maneuver you undertake. But they will give you some insight into use of the put-on, without which your manipulation cannot hope to succeed. Sure, this runs counter to basic precepts in our reborn society, like "Disdain the superficial, the pretentious. Let the true You shine through, unadorned and unaffected."

If there are fissures in your brain where this happens, you're neither effective nor attractive. You're leaking.

Identification and Credibility   The leitmotif of a put-on is, of course, credibility, and this in turn depends on riveting attention to yourself and what you are about to offer. It helps if you can develop a distinguishing *shtick*, one that not only gets and holds attention initially, but sets you apart from the mundane. This does not mean you must, or even can, master the art of the quick joke, the Bob Hope joviality, or the cocksureness of F. Lee Bailey. It does not mean putting on a Kojak approach, or even growing a Vandyke.

It means developing a talent, a quirk or two, that is not unnatural to you, that fits in with your whole personality, your attitudes, the whole "you"—one that sets you apart, that carries *identification*.

It could be the first solid step in doctoring your image for a successful put-on.

General Patton had his pearl-handled pistol, W. C. Fields his prowess with the bottle, Greta Garbo her unavailability, Jimmy Carter a melon-slice, toothy smile and a shirt-sleeve religiosity, Governor Jerry Brown his credo of "Less is more," each with his distinguishing characteristic.

It need not be grandiloquent. Even the trivial can sometimes be effective. I know a successful insurance broker who, for over twenty years, has worn a polka dot tie with a fresh bouton-niere each day. You can pick him out in any crowd. He affects an air of insouciance that is a delight to behold. Certainly there is no room for deception or bluff in this innocuous creature. And there's the young western lawyer whose *shtick* developed quite by accident. While in London he bought a suit of fine English wool with several shirts in matching color. They evoked so much com-ment on his return home, he reordered from the same shop. The image created fitted the man to perfection: quiet elegance and the veneer of success. It gave him presence and a measure of ready identification.

Superficial? Of course, but arresting, and a definite plus in his manipulative quest.

Dress habits help executives to control and direct subordi-nates, salesmen to boost sales, and trial lawyers to win cases. So runs the theory of a haberdashery engineer, John T. Molloy of New York City:

"At his suggestion, the owner of an insurance agency in a Boston suburb replaced his flashily attired sales force with men in grey suits, simple ties and button-down collars—and sales boomed. A trial lawyer with a folksy courtroom manner and a losing record was persuaded to abandon his pin-striped suits and wide-rimmed spectacles (which were more suitable for a remote 'authority figure') in favor of solid blue suits and glasses with thicker frames that gave a friendlier image. He is now winning more cases."[4]

Wardrobe engineering, says Molloy, "is just putting to-gether the elements of psychology, fashion, sociology, and art." A neat theory, perhaps too simplistic. But it has a measure of credi-bility.

Still, there are so many imponderables in shaping a charac-ter that oozes believability. The world is full of *schleppers* who, defying every convention of dress and behavior, have sharpened winning techniques in the manipulative arts.

I remember a placard in a fashionable tailoring shop: "The man who gets ahead *always* acts and looks like the man who is ahead." Don't bank on it.

The trick, obviously, is to mine your own lode and refine whatever you dig up. Mort Sahl's quiet, jerky style would suit John Wayne's God-like utterances like a size 34 on a 42. Be realistic in doctoring your image. If you're a "couth and culture" nut, with a degree in anthropology, don't try the role of Archie Bunker to make your score. Nor does it make sense to attempt a Warren Beatty maneuver when underneath you're Walter Mitty; you'll look foolish and quickly turn off whomever you're addressing.

If you were an aggressor or bully in school, you will instinctively cut the same pattern in later life, until you meet someone more aggressive or bullying. And if you made your score in earlier years by cunning, flattery, or contrived weakness, you will later develop a repertoire of maneuvers in the same mould.

Moral: No matter what size shoes you wear, or how wide or ungainly, don't try walking in someone else's. Your limp will be seen a mile away.

Within these parameters anyone can maneuver a put-on of sorts, provided he keeps in mind the basic premise: without credibility, whatever manipulation you attempt will be a juiceless effort.

Believability: What an amorphous, elusive quality, so wondrous to behold, so difficult to create or define, yet so necessary to play a winning role in the game of deception or bluff!

It shone bright on Jack Kennedy, but barely flickered for Richard Nixon. Barbara Walters and Walter Cronkite bathe in its glow. Gerald Ford tries hard with his fumbling, honest-Joe approach, but barely reaches above the back burner.

Sociological studies may tend to show that, pound for pound, the tall, smooth-looking guy has the cutting edge in getting his point across. Look at the presidents of AT&T, IT&T, or Xerox. But this doesn't mean you have to crawl into a hole if you're short, lumpy, or pockmarked. After all, Charles Bronson doesn't take a back seat in believability or likability. Neither did Golda Meir. And if you look around you, or watch the TV characters oozing machismo, you'll appreciate that it isn't necessary to be six feet tall and built like a Bronco halfback to draw and hold attention.

There are physical characteristics and vocal and social mannerisms that you carry around with you and are hard to shed. Unless they are positively repulsive, leave them alone. Regard them as just another wart you're burdened with and must accept.

If you end up with a lemon, make lemonade.

The Intellectual Veneer   So you crave an easy familiarity with matters academic—or a reasonable facsimile thereof: the expertise that lifts you from the realm of the clod, makes you a better conversationalist at cocktail parties or social gatherings, or gives you an edge with that brainy blonde with a college degree. A few suggestions:

1. Read religiously the book review section of your Sunday newspaper. Familiarize yourself with a few of the major books reviewed, their theme and general content, noting particularly the criticisms of the reviewer. This will give you a passing familiarity with events in the book world—no less profound than the views parroted around you. Few people actually read all the books they talk about. Faking is rampant, more than you imagine. And don't just say you read the book. You *re-read* it.

2. Look in the back of your dictionary and make up a list of foreign words and phrases, a few basics that you can use anywhere, anytime, like: *contretemps* for a bad mistake, *bonsoir* for good evening, *bonjour* for good morning or good day, *bon ami* for good friend, *grand merci* for many thanks, *coup d'etat,* a master stroke. And when you are in a restaurant, don't ask for the bill, it's *L'addition,* and don't call someone an upstart or jerk, he's a *parvenu.* When you lift your glass in a toast, forget the plebian "bottoms up," try *à vôtre santé,* to your good health.

3. Practice the art of "contrary opinion," the more contrary the better. If you can't readily dig up something contrary to say, learn how to leave the beaten path in your comments, whether it's *politics:* "There are no definitive solutions, today's master stroke is tomorrow's blunder"; *theatre:* "The play reeks of aesthetic impoverishment"; or *world affairs:* "Unfortunately his impact is minimal, like any man who knows the price of everything and the value of nothing."

4. Select a little-known work by a famous poet, dramatist or novelist, like Shakespeare's *Timon of Athens* or Dryden's *The Spanish Friar* and acquire a working familiarity with its theme. Memorize a few quotations. When the conversation veers to books or plays, casually drop your gem. Don't worry about accuracy. Your listener won't know the difference, he probably never heard of the work

you're quoting from. In the event you feel a comment is in order on a book or play they're discussing, and that *you* never heard of, try the contradictory concept, like "brilliantly presented, but poorly acted," or a "sad comedy," "a happy tragedy."

Your observations are obviously superficial, their imprint as lasting as a ball of spit on a hot stove. But they may rivet attention and give you a quick, if momentary, recognition, a veneer of profundity. You're on center stage, no mean feat in itself.

In the Beginning I often wonder what happens when someone who read *The First 60 Seconds* sits next to somebody who just finished *Winning Through Intimidation,* and one tries to out-impress the other with his put-on. No matter how carefully they follow the script, it's a sure bet in ten seconds they'll revert to type. The mouse will remain a mouse, the lion a lion. If the former tries to come on like Charles Bronson, he'll look as ersatz as the lion putting on a David Niven role.

Sure, the first contact is important, but you'll never engineer a convincing put-on with the come-ons you read in the How-to-Be-Convincing, How-to-Influence-People books that glut the market. They look good on TV and in the Dale Carnegie classes, but in the arena of everyday contacts, you'll need a different prescription to prepare your listener for the deception or bluff you have in mind.

"*Don't lose eye contact! Look with a steady gaze.*" Garbage. Drill your listener at the outset with a hard and steady gaze, and he will either turn away in embarrassment or mark you down as some kind of nut. The trick is to look at him initially as you would look at anyone else. If you're naturally a hard looker, bold and direct, let that frame your first contact. It will be no more or less effective than the shy or subdued gaze, if that's the way you normally begin a conversation.

"*To make a good impression at the start, come alive! Let the juices flow.*" Sound familiar? It's as practical as telling a midget he'll make a better impression if he stretches to six feet. Some of the most accomplished practitioners in the arts of deception and bluff are immobile in gesture and as plastic in facial expression as Mona Lisa.

These are prime pieces of nonsense in the "How to Convince," "Overcome by Intimidation," "Bubble with Enthusiasm" school. It assumes your listener is a moron, receptive to whatever you're selling, if only you overpower him with a solid dose of enthusiasm. You can cover him with it up to his eyeballs, but unless you acquire some basic skills in manipulation, it could be wasted energy.

Publishers strike a rich vein with every book they pour out on sure-fire ways to develop persuasive talents. One of the greatest frauds in the literature on human relationships is that you must develop specific traits or acquire a winning personality, dripping smiles and positive attitudes, in order to put over your point of view or function at maximum effectiveness.

How is it, then, you may ask, that the lectures on self-realization fill so many meeting rooms all over the country? The answer: naiveté, with the wish drowning out sober thought. Attend one of the newer schools for developing your full potential, listen to the toothy enthusiasts and venerable gurus, and see how "taught" gestures, speech techniques, and body movements look and sound, and marvel at the gullibility of the human race.

The simple and relatively unattractive fact is that "natural" is still the most effective, the most beautiful, ingredient in human persuasion.

> Almost all absurdity of conduct arises from the imitation of those whom we cannot resemble.
> — *Samuel Johnson*

> He does it with a better grace, but I do it more natural.[5]
> — *Shakespeare*

A man's best manner is what most becomes him. In short, if you are a smiler, smile. If you're not, don't put it on. A row of shiny teeth won't project conviction or warmth, if it isn't framed by what you say, how you say it, and the whole "you."

Try moving up to a dog with a crinkly smile on your face and fear or hostility boiling inside you. He'll instinctively sense the phoniness of your approach. Then drop the smile and make warm, friendly sounds and reassuring gestures. See the difference. He might even lick your hand.

But that doesn't mean you can't improve your image. The "you" that your family finds comfortable might be less than endearing to a stranger. There's a point where "being yourself" can be positively obnoxious to others. If you read this chapter carefully, you'll see the line between *sharpening the natural "you"* and acting out another's script.

Does it matter you are not Vladimir Horowitz? Nobody complains that Leonard Bernstein is not Toscanini.

Look at the contrasting make-up of three leaders at the trial bar, all masters in the art of oral manipulation.

Melvin Belli, now a portly white-haired figure, hides a razor-sharp mind and a fantastic Niagara of energy behind a grandiloquent manner. A pedantic or pontifical air would be as transparent as the ebullience of a middle-aged juvenile.

F. Lee Bailey, a self-assured bantam cock and in my opinion one of the most able criminal lawyers in the country, has an uncanny ability to project an air of outraged innocence before a jury. Low-keyed, perfectly controlled, he zeros in on gut issues with deadly accuracy. The combative underdog role fits him to perfection.

Louis Nizer is the kindly, unassuming patriarch of the American bar. Before metropolitan juries who regard lawyers with a jaundiced eye, this slight, *nebbish*-like man with the benign manner and soft speech, is almost unbeatable.

Conviction rides on self-esteem, an awareness of your competence to do what you set out to do. This awareness won't spring from half-baked notions of the kind of person you would dearly love to be.

It must have its roots in a calculated appraisal of the person you really are. Unless you can accept this person—warts and all—you are not developing your manipulative capacity to the fullest. You're unconsciously borrowing from others the traits and mannerisms you admire and would like to make your own. It simply can't be done. You may succeed in building a façade of sorts, but that's all it will be—a façade, and in the arena of human contacts, and in the practice of the Machiavellian arts of deception or bluff, as unrewarding as the lower half of a mermaid.

Here are a few suggestions, born out of long experience as a trial lawyer, for making a good start:

1. Since initial impressions may play a role, even if minor, do and say whatever you would naturally do or say to someone you like. If it's someone who instantly turns you off, act out the role or abandon the quest. The put-on must be one that wears well and looks natural. You'll make your score easier and quicker by acting out your own script, however loud, aggressive, or humbling it may be, provided the actor is *the natural, not awkwardly contrived* YOU, without the prickling barbs of one-upmanship.

2. If all you elicit is a Buddha inscrutability or if your listener, by a wandering gaze, shows inattention, you could be in trouble. Switch to verbal stroking. (See Chapter 9.)

3. Don't begin by asking questions that run to the core of your ultimate goal. It creates defensiveness at the outset.

4. Stay loose, never dogmatic, so you can shape your put-on to the responses you get.

Judging others, and appraising their susceptibility to the manipulations you have in mind, presents a real problem. There are no fixed guidelines. Your judgment will be instinctive at best. But there is one criterion—recently popularized—that I urge you to reject.

> A great nose shows a
> Great man
> Genial, courteous,
> Intellectual,
> Virile, courageous.[6]
> ———————————————— *Edmond Rostand*

You can no more judge a person's susceptibility to your manipulative efforts by his facial characteristics than by his body build. Listen to this profundity by a lecturer that I recently heard:

"If you see sad lines on your listener's face, you have a tough customer, hard as hell to persuade. Watch out for those vertical creases."

Tight lips are said to give the same signal. A full-lipped

individual, on the other hand, is described as warm, sympathetic, more likely to accept what you offer.

Pure hokum.

Some more cogent advice:

"Beware of people who have gloomy eyes, with extra white showing. They're harder to convince."

"Shifty eyes show a lack of intention to follow through on what is promised."

"Glassy, bloodshot eyes denote unpredictability, unreliability."

And here are pearls of wisdom from a popular face-reading authority:

"Slender men tend to be sensitive, intellectually active, emotional, have well-developed imaginative and creative powers."

"Face readers agree with the commonly held belief that a low narrow forehead is generally a sign indicating irresponsibility, carelessness, dishonesty and in many cases, brutality. . . . About the only legitimate profession in which such men sometimes reach high position is that of *politics*."

High-sounding garbage.

In my early days at the trial bar, I formed an instinctive fear of the tight-lipped, Calvinistic type of witness or juror. He would be the toughest to reach. He would see only white and black, never the greys, the most fertile area for lawyers. I soon discovered this was pure bunk. Any seasoned trial lawyer will tell you, for example, that he judges a witness's susceptibility to the deceptions and bluffs of cross-examination by an instinctive appraisal of the *whole person*.

And that is precisely how you should judge the object of your manipulation.

Flora Davis, the knowledgeable author of *Inside Intuition*, concludes that "the face does not express emotion in a reliably recognizable way." Even so with body motions; she points out that both fall into the realm of speculation.

Davis states that after her extensive study of the subject, she learned that "nonverbal communication is more than just a system of emotional cues and that it can't, in fact, really be separated from verbal communication. The two are woven together inextricably, for when human beings meet face to face, they communicate simultaneously on many levels, conscious and subconscious. And then they integrate all that by using the decoding device that's sometimes called the sixth sense: Intuition."[7]

I submitted six photographs, showing different facial types, to two psychologist friends. In not one instance did their interpretations match as to which person would be least, or most, likely to succumb to the wiles of another.

> In point of fact, what is interesting about people in good society . . . is the mask that each one of them wears, not the reality behind the mask. It is humiliating confession, but we are all of us made out of the same stuff. Where we differ from each other is purely in accidentals; in personal appearance, tricks of habit and the like. The more one analyzes people, the more all reasons for analysis disappear. Sooner or later one comes to that dreadful universal thing called human nature.
>
> ———————————— *Oscar Wilde: The Decay of Lying*

Paul Ekman, another first-rate authority on nonverbal communication, commented that "human appearance, and especially the face, constitutes as tight a package of innumerable contributing variables as might be found anywhere in cognition research."

3. The Executive Masquerade

And it must be understood that a prince, and especially a new prince, cannot observe all those things which are considered good in men, being often obliged, in order to maintain the state, to act against faith, against charity, against religion. And, therefore, he must have a mind disposed to adapt itself according to the wind, and as the variations of fortune dictate, and as I said before, not deviate from what is good, *if possible*.

— *Machiavelli*

Domination By Deception

> The look of sincerity in those pale eyes was so perfectly
> convincing that I knew myself to be in the presence of a
> truly deceitful man.[1]
> ———————————————— *Gore Vidal: 1876*

You crave more recognition, a more sharply defined role in your
executive position. There is much you can learn from the put-ons
used by the managerial community to deceive or bluff their way
to a stronger power base. They range from the trivial to the
grandiloquent, the credible to the childishly pretentious.

From my own observations, the manipulations and deceptions that prevail in corporate in-fighting, make it a jungle,
largely inpenetrable to the outer world, with far more traps than
found in the academic or professional worlds. Incidentally, the
male gender is used throughout this discussion, not with the
intent to exclude the female executive, who can be as rapacious,
abrasive, or charmingly deceptive as her male counterpart, but
merely to avoid the silly and cumbersome device of "he/she"
"chairman/chairlady," or "person."

The Game Plan   In the unlikely event you are in the class of
C. C. Garvin (Exxon) $696,000 annually; or Irving Shapiro (Du-
Pont) $668,000, you will have no interest in, much less a need for,
suggestions on how to dominate your subordinates by deception.
But for the rest of the managerial community, at the middle or
close to the top levels, the stratagems suggested here may have
more than a passing interest, particularly where the area of the
throne is beset with intrigues, conflicting ambitions, or dissension
in the ranks.

The stratagems, suggested by a wide range of managers,
run the gamut from intimidation to decimation of those below
and around the throne. The name of the game is control by
manipulation. Usually unobtrusive. Outwardly friendly. Like an
arm wrapped around your shoulder—the knife carefully concealed.

If you decide upon this course, your maneuvers should
give no signal of your ultimate goal, or the play immediately

ahead. It's not unlike the feints and ruses of a quarterback who will appear to pass the ball to a teammate but actually keep it, or run in one direction and then veer sharply in another, adopting deceptive stances throughout the game—all aimed at diverting attention and clearing the track to the desired goal, which in your case is complete control of your territory.

A variety of manipulations create and enhance the dominant role. It helps, for example, if at the inception of your relationship with the company, you avoided a precise description of your duties.

The conventional statement of responsibilities and duties limits your discretionary powers, and could prove a barrier to carrying out new projects. The less specificity the better. The ideal arrangement is one that allows you wide rein as administrator or manager of your department or division, with plenty of room to maneuver in directions not likely to win approval at the time of your hiring.

And don't draw conclusions from the title they give you, particularly if you are an executive in a hurry, impatient with snail-like advancements, over-aware of the short life span in the corporate ranks (set at 40, old at 50, expendable at 60). Corporate semantics is replete with deceptions. You may find yourself in the position of a hunter lost in the woods, armed with a high-powered Winchester loaded with blanks. Traditionally an administrator coordinates operations and issues directives, but lacks authority to fire. A manager hires *and* fires. The distinction is important. The title is not.

There is almost no limit to the maneuvers available to the track-wise executive. He has acquired an instinctive awareness of what feeds the ego or establishes a strong rapport, as well as a perception of what to avoid in his dealings with those at the top of the pyramid.

He will not, for example, offer a façade of strong independence to one he knows prefers the submissive, agreeable role in those under him—anymore than he would play pussycat to a top dog who has made it clear he admires creativity and outspokenness. In no event will he present a course of action, or make a suggestion, likely to reflect adversely on a superior or prove abrasive in carrying out company policies.

Deception is the homage that artifice pays to virtue.

The aspiring and knowledgeable executive will instinctively trim his sails to whatever course helps to establish his dominance, deferring to the incompetent, ego-hungry, or power-obsessed superior where such deference enhances his image.

He will develop a hound-dog tenacity in ferreting out the likes, dislikes, and idiosyncracies of those in a position to polish that image—as well as identifying those in the power circle, those on the periphery, and the pretenders, those with impressive job titles but meaningless roles. Like the white-haired, senatorial-looking figure described to me by a General Electric executive a few years ago:

"His title is top rank, and his high-sounding rhetoric has the ring of papal infallibility. But it contributes zero to company policy. Purely decorative, no more weight than a sprig of parsley on a plate of hors-d'oeuvres."

I know one enterprising executive who carefully cultivated the widow of a majority stockholder in the company. He discovered her passion for antique clocks. It was no big deal for him to study the history of clocks, even buying a few antiques that he contributed to her collection. She found in him a kindred soul, establishing a communion of sorts and creating a link in the executive's chain of top-level supporters, never suspecting that he had no more interest in her antiques than in the hieroglyphs of the ancient Egyptians.

No less enterprising is the tactic of an executive I met in my travels across the country, bright and thirtyish, who grew quickly from smart to smartass. His power base was a cozy relationship that he established with the executive head of a major customer.

Their common interest was tennis, played at an almost professional level. Recurrent complaints from his friend about service and quality suddenly found a receptive ear. Thus fortified, he moved ahead fast, setting somewhat of a track record. "A pushy bastard," one of his colleagues remarked. "Cocky as hell. If he has a friend in the entire organization, I have yet to find him."

His game plan was simple, no different from that commonly encountered in corporate in-fighting: to screw whomever he could, to make amends profusely if he drew blood, to plan his next maneuver immediately, to execute it with dispatch, learning from the previous move, and so on, until he reached the peak of the pyramid, when he demanded absolute fairness and integrity from all under his command. His expression, formerly as communicative as a Picasso abstract, was now warm and open.

This was his final absolution, his rebirth to nobility, the Devil cheated and Heaven won.

That Florentine sage of duplicity, Niccolo Machiavelli, posed and answered the question "whether it is better to be loved than feared, or the reverse. The answer is, of course, that it would be best to be both loved and feared. But since the two rarely come together, anyone compelled to choose will find greater security in being feared than in being loved. For this can be said about the generality of men: that they are ungrateful, fickle, dissembling, anxious to flee danger, and covetous of gain."

Protecting Your Rear   Don't assume that the assistants you select will serve you loyally and unselfishly, without chicanery, as long as you treat them with respect and keep your distance. You don't hold a copyright on the put-ons and deceptions that raised you from the common herd. A safe maneuver is to hire only those who give promise of filling the role of a hard-working drone. They will never threaten your position and may even enhance your exposure by contrast. But management may later see through your stratagem and call you to task, unless you can convince them that your selections are doing a good job and learning fast under your patient guidance.

Another safeguard to protect your rear is to hire assistants who are bright and ambitious, placing them in situations where they must compete with each other for your favor. It's a delicate balance at best. They must be smart enough to carry a good part of your work load, but not smart enough to appraise you as a big put-on. Moreover, your manipulations must not raise their hopes too fast or too high, lest your scenario become a transparent fraud. Your role must always remain that of the patient Great White Father, impartial and all-knowing, to whom they can turn with their endless stream of ideas, complaints, and drivel. By adroit manipulation, this script can be played out indefinitely, the leader relying on the fears and ambitions of his subordinates to control each situation that may arise, even to creating confusion where necessary to assure that only he knows what is actually happening.

The ideal protection, of course, is the competent but unambitious backstop, the nine to fivers who never raise their sights beyond a steady paycheck, who are content to "cut the wood and carry the water pail." They stay well within the niche carved for them, offering no threats to your authority and respecting the façade of competency and wisdom you have so patiently built. If their output is not brilliant, at least it is steady and generally better than your own, yet not so outstanding that you can't take full or partial credit for what they accomplish.

Masking Incompetence or Mediocrity

> It is a sad truth that a leader who does the wrong things in the right way, will up to a certain point, gain greater allegiance and enjoy more success than one who does the right things in the wrong way.[2]
>
> ——————————————— Desmond Morris: The Human Zoo

The first rule is never to reveal too much of yourself, lest you expose the chasm that passes for competency. It's not too difficult to create the illusion you have the solution to a problem that arises. Cultivate the easy-going, benign manner and smile that lessens the urgency of a crisis that comes under discussion.

Hold back enough of yourself so that your subordinates or superiors are never quite certain what course you will take, or what you will say, in any given situation. You can hide a tower of mediocrity behind your imperturbability and slight mysteriousness.

Occasionally, do and say the unexpected. Enlarge the trivial—about which you feel comfortable—to a larger dimension, but only when you can talk on it with some degree of authority. Watch for the opportunity to strengthen that Mysterious Image by moving the conversation to yourself and whatever credentials you have, however meager, like the marketing coup you pulled off in your previous position.

But don't go beyond vague impressions in your personal life, unless it's something only an idiot would hide, like the M.B.A.

you got at M.I.T., or your millionaire uncle who married a Du-Pont. Never forget, however, that once the others have squeezed you dry of things to know about yourself, you've become just one of them, stark naked in your commonality. I'm not counseling concealment or lying, merely cultivation of the habit of evasion, of talking without communicating on matters you're not too familiar with, or prefer not to discuss, rather than risk revealing your own inadequacy.

While it is true that corporate managers eventually rise to the level of their own incompetence, the duration of their tenancy can be extended indefinitely by judicious use of a few manipulative tactics.

A client of mine, the stooped and aging head of a large tool corporation in which he was the majority stockholder, had an overriding ambition to groom his son as successor. The offspring had all the accoutrements of the upbeat executive, from the elegant pin-striped suit to his blue-grey tinted glasses. And he fingered his gold Cartier pencil with the authority of a conductor on the podium.

The youth, an affable and handsome sort, was not averse to the plan, but unfortunately was more suited to the job of ski instructor or manager of a Latin American resort than a corporate decision maker. Yet he was clever enough to hide his limitations behind an ingenious web of deception and bluff. He proved a master of the great put-on, talking at meetings just enough to maintain visibility, yet saying nothing anyone could remember and offending nobody. I noticed how careful he was to avoid half-assed dissertations on subjects he was only vaguely familiar with.

The young man seemed to recognize instinctively the power rituals at director's meeting or committee conferences, the importance of respecting self-created images or symbols of authority, and the comparative ease with which his mediocrity could maintain its comfortable level. Among his favorite contributions where opposing views were presented and some response on his part was called for:

"This needs a little more input."

"It's too important for a quick decision. I can see a lot of problems if we go off half-cocked."

"There's merit in both points of view. I've got to give it a little more thought."

The ability to mask his density in perception was indeed a miracle to behold. I recall a board discussion involving methods of financing a projected acquisition. The Old Man turned expectantly to his son when it came his turn to express an opinion.

"I'd vote for Jim's plan. [A satisfied look from Jim to the offspring of the majority stockholder.] It has considerable merit in view of our past experiences in financing acquisitions. And I'm not qualifying that opinion with any 'buts' or 'on the other hand.' All I ask before we reach a final decision is for Art to give us a little more detail on the reasons for his opposition. Or even better, a memo for a more in-depth discussion at our next meet. How about it, Art?"

No intimation that the speaker's bird-brain couldn't comprehend what the plan was all about. He bruised no egos, made no waves, not even a ripple. He knew that a direct reply or dissent might easily expose the void that passed for understanding.

The longevity of your bluff is variable, depending on the link between the bluffee and the throne.

I know another manager, the son of a major customer who aspired to executive rank. But his heart and mind belonged to a different kind of business, less competitive, less bruising, notwithstanding his coveted M.B.A. degree from Stanford. For a time he hid his ineptitude behind a simple maneuver which I recommend to managers unsure of corporate semantics.

He thoroughly memorized stock responses to basic problems likely to emerge at staff meetings, parroting them as if freshly minted; problems like how to reduce year-to-year fluctuations in sales, or how to orient operations to insure a better performance in rate of return on capital investment. The rationale for his deception was simple enough. As he once confided to me when I asked him about the practical effect of a new government regulation on his department's production:

"You're asking the wrong man. That's the kind of decision I duck or pass on. I'm not kidding myself. I keep visible, make my figures visible. I like to think I energize, stimulate. If an audience has no representation on stage, the show looks dull, flat." He was on stage for a longer period than I anticipated. Then his glibness became transparent and he sank to his true level.

Mediocrity hides behind a myriad of put-ons, woven of a variety of deceptions, of varying degrees of detectability. I know another director, a hearty greeter type, who sits on a prestigious bank's executive committee by virtue of the extensive investments his family controls. His knowledge of finance, at best superficial and not enough to fill a flea's navel, is given an illusion of depth by his uncanny ability to come up with an aphorism or witticism appropriate to almost every problem under discussion. *Bartlett's Familiar Quotations* replaced *Basic Banking Problems*.

> Gratiano speaks an infinite deal of nothing. . . . His reasons are as two grains of wheat hid in two bushels of chaff; you shall seek all day ere you find them, and when you have them, they are not worth the search.[3]
> ———————————————— *Shakespeare*

Staff meetings always pose problems for mediocrities, particularly when they're confronted with a crisis situation calling for some participation. The obvious strategy is to *wordize*. It can be banal, or so general as to be trivial in content, the kind of message a pigeon could carry on one wing. And when the meeting is over, and someone asks what was discussed, or what decisions reached, simply reply:

"It was a productive session. The problems in our division were really clarified. We can see them more clearly now. All views were aired. There were a few points I would have liked to bring up, but they were covered so thoroughly I saw no need to prolong the meeting."

"What points?" you may be asked. Your reply is straightforward. Select a few of the suggestions that were approved and offer them as your own. Nobody will know or care that you're riding piggyback on another's output and sharing in the credit.

> Men almost always walk in paths beaten by others and act by imitation. Though he cannot hold strictly to the ways of others or match the ability of those he imitates, a prudent man must always tread the path of great men and imitate those who have excelled, so that even if his ability does not match theirs, at least he will achieve some semblance of it.
> ———————————————— *Machiavelli*

The Great Put-On not only camouflages mediocrities, it can fix them in positions of relative security in the corporate structure, like assistant to a vice-president, since they generally offer small threat to their immediate superiors. The role they play is usually ceremonial, such as conducting important visitors through the plant, cutting ribbons, sitting behind an executive officer at a board meeting and handing him documents he calls for, and performing a myriad of duties aimed principally at polishing the image of the master or relieving him of menial tasks.

The trained eye can readily spot them entering staff conferences or board meetings, like a procession of doges in ancient Venice, leading a retinue of satraps. And when discussion opens, these dutiful members of the family are the first to voice approval of proposals submitted from above, like paid claques in an opera house.

To the outside world they're presented as imposing figures, often with impressive titles. J. Walter Thompson, one of the world's largest advertising agencies, recently listed 145 vice-presidents, 4 executive vice-presidents, and 8 senior vice-presidents.

"A good quarter are deadwood, and many of the others are no more than ceremonial," a staff member in a competitive agency told me. "But they all either have strong pipelines to important clients or have learned the art of keeping the drones under them happy and productive."

An old friend who is an important decision maker in a large Western corporation introduced me to the Falstaff figure of his assistant. When he left, my friend commented: "He fills in for me at some of the conventions. The man's got charm to spare. When he turns it on, I swear he can sell anybody, anything, anytime. His talk to our newly hired executives is like an aphrodisiac. The enthusiasm it whips up is a miracle to behold. 'America likes winners. It craves and worships winners. That should be your goal in meeting projections. Believe me, friends, coming in No. 1 is the sweetest. Does anyone remember who flew the Atlantic second, or who discovered America second?'

"But it's all glitter, a big put-on. He's conned everyone in the company into thinking he knows all about my divison—all except me. Do you know, Syd, I'm so damned tired of these conventions, the rubbery steaks, watered-down Martinis, the hogwash you have to listen to, that if my charm boy did nothing but front for me, he'd earn his pay three times over?"

"Does he ever deliver your speech?" I asked.

"No, he can usually make up a neat talk of his own, full of the usual crap you hear at conventions, about how innovative our company is, or the bright future of the industry if we had less government control. But if anyone should ask him for an opinion on industry practices or other gut level matters, he'd do one of two things: fall flat on his face, or bury what he's saying in a sea of words and phrases like you've never heard—most likely the latter. I do recall one instance where he was pressed for an answer to a real gutsy question about our operations; that fat face fell, dissolving into an expression that reminded you of a wedding cake left out in the rain."

Many persons in the corporate community who have risen to middle- or low-level managerial responsibility are committed to the stance of the Big Smile, the vise-like handshake, the kind of friendliness that wraps around you like a warm embrace. Their faces are fixed in a permanent mould of cheerfulness. Like the Delphic oracle, they are all things to all men, unfailingly agreeable.

They find it difficult to bring themselves to a posture of disagreement or critical evaluation—not because their acuity has atrophied under its permanent umbrella of sunshine, but because they are never at ease in any position except that of agreeability. Even a moment's digression might drop the mask and reveal them as weaklings, playing the game of the big put-on, or the big bluff.

The gambits you can use to hide your mediocrity are infinite, depending on your ingenuity. I know a sales and promotion manager in a large midwest plant who was frustrated by his inability to improve the mix of his company's products or lift sales to higher levels. His pace was pedestrian, compared to the flow of new product ideas from his company's competitors. He inserted an advertisement in the Help Wanted columns of a local newspaper for experienced copywriters, offering a top position with a "unique opportunity for the right man."

Out of the swarm of replies he selected the most promising

and arranged interviews. Each applicant was told the nature of the company's operations and then given an assignment.

"How would you prepare copy for marketing any one or more of our products? What would you conceive as possible diversifications?"

A stream of fresh ideas dropped into his lap, offering a convenient cover for his own mediocrity. The brain-picking worked for a time, until the man he hired recognized the handiwork of several friends who had applied for the same job. That put an end to the deception and to his job as sales-promotion manager.

> . . . for the old fashioned notion of principle, he has substi-
> tuted a new idea, that of the primary importance of smart-
> ness, i.e., of that quality which enables a man to get ahead
> of his fellow men by shortcuts, dodges, tricks, devices of all
> kinds which just fall short of crime.[4]
> ——————————— *Heroes and Heroines of Fiction*

The head of the Western division of a large food-processing company rose from the ranks of department managers largely because of his ability to institute innovative production procedures and, as he put it, "cure corporate constipation."

But his talents were imbedded in deviousness, the better to hide his mediocrity. He was a master at the carefully contrived deception. He regularly plucked the brains of his subordinates by encouraging wide expression of ideas at staff meetings, draining imaginations for cost-cutting suggestions, rewarding contributors, even encouraging lively disagreement among subordinates.

He labored over all submissions with a skill honed to perfection, rephrasing, revising, rewriting those with the most promise, often condensing several into one. They all bore his imprimatur in progress reports to company headquarters in the East. To the higher echelons of management, he was a highly original, imaginative executive, destined for greater responsibilities.

So ask yourself, if you are an executive at the middle level, anxious to polish your image and somewhat dubious about your ability to cope:

1. *Are there wells I can tap, systematically and unobtrusively, always "for the good of the company"?* Look for the Over-Achiever, hungry for recognition or promotion. You are more likely to strike pay dirt with his input than that of the drone. Avoid the too-brilliant; he is the one most likely to penetrate the facade and recognize his own handiwork, reading between the lies, no matter how carefully you mingle them with the truths. You may have to dig deep for the right combination of moderate intelligence and high originality; rarely will one appear without some vestige of the other. Fortunately, the latter does not depend upon, or always grow full-blown from, the former.

2. *Do I have, or can I learn, the art of altering what others contribute, so that the end product bears little or no resemblance to the original?* The pretense of originality must, of course, be kept credible at all times. Lapses that reveal its ersatz nature could blow your whole game plan.

3. And, most important, *Can I accept wholeheartedly and without qualification Balzac's precept that "there is no absolute virtue, it is all a matter of circumstance"?*

But, you may well ask, how long will a board of directors tolerate mediocrity in you? Longer than you think. The directors are usually friends of the chief executive, put there to preserve his position or enhance corporate prestige. They may ask routine questions, make a few innocuous suggestions, but rarely play the role of hound dog. In the absence of a catastrophic situation (as a lawsuit against the corporation, officers *and* directors, or a disastrous balance sheet) they make no waves. One chief executive remarked: "Our meetings traditionally follow a catered lunch, with cocktails, in the board room. The atmosphere is relaxed, friendly. We're one family."

So don't be swayed by the eye-boggling credentials of corporate directors, and don't expect they will bring their expertise to board meetings to question the judgment of their friend. Their doodlings on the pad placed in front of them is often the sum total of what they leave behind.

The Innovator

> Most deceivers are cursed at not because we despise their
> deceptions, but because we envy their success at deceiv-
> ing.

To most junior executives, scoring by deception or bluff is a new,
and often awesome, experience. But, if judicially applied, it's
worth the effort. It may not help your quest for greater recognition, but it sure as hell won't hurt it.

A few suggestions, born of a wide range of experiences by
those in the managerial community:

Look for problem areas in company operations, such as
below-quota figures in sales or production, excessive turnovers in
management or labor, or dismal profits in the last quarter. Create
a few innovative approaches to the problem, even if it means
studying the operations of corporate competitors, so you can use
them as a basis for your own presentation. Reduce your ideas to
appropriate form, whether graphs, line drawings, or charts, the
more visual and complex the better.

Remember, you're not hoping for acceptance of your
suggestions (which you sense is most unlikely), but simply for
more exposure for yourself.

A junior executive in a large mail order organization con-
structs monthly diagrammatic trees, with branches representing
marketing areas and offshoots in red indicating problem spots.
At the end of each branch are approximations of gross future
sales, raised above current figures. Numbers refer to legends at
the bottom of the chart, describing the thrusts of competitors in
each area and opportunities for expansion of existing sales
techniques.

To the casual viewer, Junior has researched the field down
to the bare bone, marrying risk to maximum gain in each marketing area. Impressive, but contrived. More show than substance.

A newly hired executive with a flair for innovation
sounded off at a staff conference of a client corporation:

"I've studied our operations carefully and a few thoughts
come to mind, even though I'm comparatively new with the
company. We lack a single image. Everything we do, from office

stationery to signs, brochures, and advertisements, lacks a single visible impact."

He was grandiloquent, but when someone asked him "What specific image do you have in mind?" he sank in a sea of words:

"We're in a highly competitive field, building and selling the highest-priced product in its field. We should integrate all the visual elements into an impressive image of corporate integrity. That's what we need to give us more clout, a stronger competitive edge."

Impressive, but no more than Dale Carnegie rhetoric. Still, he raised himself a niche higher than the twenty others that were present. To some of them, the speaker was a "I-Can-Do-It-Better-Guy," the tricky kind of guy that climbs corporate ladders two rungs at a time. He could have made a better imprint if he came prepared with a layout. But I suspect that was beyond his midget brain.

Which suggests two caveats: First, if the large problems are beyond your grasp, the minuscule may serve your purpose, like a new logo or more attractive advertising masthead. Whatever will sharpen the corporate image is a likely target.

Second, be sure your brainchild reaches the right desk. Avoid your immediate superior, who may make himself co-author, or bury your idea in his graveyard file: For Future Reference. Sure, he'll stamp you a first-class bastard, and a threat to his own security, when he learns you've over-reached. But "nice guys" don't finish last in the race for recognition in the corporate jungle; they never leave the starting line.

But the coin has two sides. Before you try your hand at manipulating an innovation, look over the field. The roadblocks could be set so solid and the jungle beset with so many pitfalls that you may well decide to play Mr. Br'er Rabbit and use deception to *hide* your sharpness. True, it's far less dramatic, less rewarding in the short run, but it has advantages in that type of situation.

A remarkable book by Alan Harrington, *Life in the Crystal Palace,* points out that a real or pretended lack of creative ability could be a talent in itself, a positive asset in the corporate hierarchy. No matter how many times the top level changes policies, the man without a solid idea remains unaffected. He bruises no egos. He goes strictly by The Book, which Harrington describes as a

covenant developed by "mediocre people to frighten outlaws."
The outlaw is the original man.

So don't play the Heroic Outlaw by flashing your bright
and shining ideas, if the terrain is so tricky it could land you flat on
your back.

The Hiring Strategy   "If a teacher you become, by your pupils
you'll be taught." No less true: if an executive you become, by
your subordinates you'll be screwed, unless you follow a simple
strategy in the hiring process.

As remarked by a Midwest executive: "When I look
through the personnel records for a replacement as my immediate subordinate, I search for the mediocre performer. For
two practical reasons. They are least likely to begin breathing on
my back, and the last to demand substantial salary increases. They
subsist quite nicely on a diet of small raises and big titles."

Obviously, what he feared was too outstanding a performance record, one that could flaunt talents he lacked.

> He who causes another to become powerful, ruins himself,
> for he brings such a power into being either by design or
> force, and both of these elements are suspect to the one he
> has made powerful.
>
> ———————————————————————— *Machiavelli*

Under no circumstances will you invite a challenge to your position by training a strong No. 2 man in the full range of your duties
and responsibilities, the supercharged, adrenalin-flooded type.
He could prove a Trojan horse if your alliances in the company
structure weaken, or if perchance he develops the same ambition
and deviousness that put you in your present position. Where you
delegate authority, there are three simple rules to follow: don't
give too much at one time, limit it to specific and well-defined
areas, and, most important, maintain control.

It helps to offer an occasional carrot in the form of slight
pay increases or increased responsibilities, conditioned always
upon doing whatever you decide will tighten that control. And
when it comes to promotions, forget "The Best Man for the Job."
In company politics, even the neophyte knows this is an axiom

honored more in the breach than in the observance. The overriding consideration is always "What's best strategically for me?"

The Promotion Process   Promotions can be used as manipulative levers in maintaining tighter control of your subordinates. Generating rumors about likely prospects, expanding the list of prospects to maximum size, subtly creating hope and anxiety, even though you have already made your decision, will accomplish two things: reinforce your status as No. 1, The Man in Charge, and compel a sort of feudal loyalty in the hope of suitable reward at a later date.

The Over-Achiever.   When you are No. 1 in your division, you sooner or later meet with the Over-Achiever, over whom you cannot, for a variety of reasons, maintain too tight a control. It's not always easy to slake his thirst for performance without reflecting on your own. And you may also sense that you won't satisfy his craving for recognition by throwing him a few status symbols, such as a new title or a larger office.

It's even possible that his track record may be so outstanding that bypassing him for a promotion would be too obvious a miscalculation.

There are a few maneuvers you can employ to cool the hot pistol—in addition to the common ploy of gradually increasing the details of his job beyond his capacity or endurance, letting him have more of the "little tats" while you keep the "big tats for yourself." Much safer are the more conventional deceptions like keeping him off important committees, giving him a desk at the far end of the office, or making him share a secretary with another executive.

These manipulations could be stillborn, with the deceivee adapting to the new environment created by the deceiver—if not happily, at least with that curious resignation typical of so many individuals. He accepts his changed status and the small humiliations with tolerance, often growing into a sort of affection for the new surroundings.

Limit his communications to your superiors, or to the board. Make it a condition of his promotion that all his reports and recommendations first land on your desk. You then have an opportunity to make enough modifications or additions to give it the appearance of a joint effort. Even better, dilute the effect by spreading the credit among others on your staff who may have made suggestions on the same subject. If he proves too unmanageable, or it appears he is aware of your deceptions, beware of over-acting.

Your shaky put-on could become too noticeable for comfort. The best ploy, if you can swallow whatever scruples you have left, is to plant the seeds of self-destruction. Assign tasks that you know are difficult, even impossible, to accomplish, fix tight completion dates. Exploit whatever weaknesses you can discover. If, for example, you find that he is a sexual acrobat, give him a secretary or female assistant that you know has the same proclivity, so that any resulting hanky-panky will justify his demotion or dismissal.

As a last resort, if all other deceptions fail, consider eliminating his job in the corporate structure by tightening the budget in your division or department, or distributing his duties among others—always, of course, in the best interests of the company. Outright dismissal is major surgery, with all its attendant risks. It is occasionally justified for a variety of reasons, depending on the ingenuity of the executive wielding the axe: disruptiveness (in contrived situations that would tax the patience of a dozen saints), low productivity (in meeting impossible sales or production targets), or poor leadership (a catchall euphemism where no other reason is readily available, as informative as "incompatible").

The managing editor of a trade publication described to me how he hired "this pushy genius fresh out of college. It wasn't long before I pegged him as conniving, abrasive, over-ambitious. Now, I like hard workers dedicated to their job, but he was just too much of a good thing. It was hard as hell to contain him. I put his desk in Siberia, far away from the other editors. I gave him assignments that kept him out of the mainstream for weeks at a time, then chopped his reports to pieces. He was kept off committees, his name rarely appeared alone, usually in conjunction with another editor. Fortunately, he got the message and moved to another publication. The man just wasn't cut for the role of acolyte, content to sit at the altar of his Father Superior."

I know a division manager in a western New York plant, so frustrated by a pushy, over-qualified No. 2, that he developed a bad case of ulcerative colitis. None of the conventional hatchet techniques seemed appropriate. The stratagem he finally selected had a deceptive simplicity.

He secured permission from the executive vice-president for an evaluation of all nineteen subordinates under his command, using his own aptitude and psychometric tests to assess attitudes, psychological status, performance, and job compatibility. He charted the results. Even if his No. 2 had the brain of an Einstein or the dedication of a Steinmetz, he would have made a miserable score. Under cover of this deception, it was safe to cool the over-achiever by a transfer to a dead-end position, where he posed no immediate threat. The final assessment: "over-promoted, beyond his capacity for a good adjustment, he is able to control details with reasonable speed and make a proper delegation of duties, but is totally lacking in creativity, the ability to forge new paths."

Another manager used the popular "situational test," where several imaginary characters are placed in a situation requiring exercise of a variety of talents. The replies are studied to determine how each executive responded to the problems presented. Another manager targets his victim by an "individual stress" test; the interviewer deliberately imposing pressures by contrived arguments and contradictions, basing his evaluation on the reactions he elicits.

The Sidetrack Maneuver   Now suppose your power structure appears under reasonably tight control, except for faint signs of a rising genius on your staff, restrained and deferential, with a variety of ideas, some too good for your own comfort. To ignore them would be patently defensive. To accept too many might be the beginning of an erosion of your own stature as No. 1, The Man in Charge, From Whom All Ideas Bright and New Emerge.

Here's a manipulation suggested by one knowledgeable manager. "I transferred the budding genius to another division. Gave him a new and more prestigious title. Then I selected someone as his immediate subordinate whose loyalty was to me first, the company second. I encouraged him to build his own power base, showed him how. The rest was simple."

I sat in a Holiday Inn Bar, outside San Diego, not too long

ago, discussing this stratagem with one of its victims. He sipped his drink pensively, and said with a touch of anger edged with hurt: "I didn't realize until it was too late that I'd been screwed. The high-sounding title and big office—Manager of Western Marketing—looked impressive. But it was pure crap. This assistant they sent out was meeting all our customers, recommending replacements to the Head Office, even developed new market analysis and sales projections. All under my name, of course. But his line of communication with headquarters grows warmer, mine cools. I'm getting the message, loud and clearer each day. 'Man, you're sidetracked. Derailed.' Now you tell me, where the hell do I go from here?"

The Sought-After Stratagem   So you're middle-aged and balding, with your earlier dreams fast fading in the deadening routine of your job, and the inner hierarchy of your company looking more remote and impenetrable each year. Try the sought-after stratagem, like generating rumors you're being courted by a competitor, or maneuvering a small blurb to that effect into the gossip column of a trade publication. It may work, and in any event won't hurt. There's a germ of truth in Charles Schwab's oft-quoted remark: "If nobody tries to hire away our executives, they're not as good as they or the company thinks."

     You might also consider a different put-on, one that a former client of mine manipulated to good advantage. He bought a minority position in a small chain of auto accessory stores and was given a minor managerial role. He soon envisioned an expansion into other areas, with himself the spearhead. The management and majority stockholders resisted, and suggested he look for another position. He looked, but not for a position. He took an option to buy the majority stock in a small but ailing competitor—an option he never intended to exercise. He also alerted several real estate brokers to look for store sites, near those of the chain. The word spread fast, and the bluff paid the dividend he sought. The opposition to his plans faded. A remarkable man, he now heads his own nationwide chain of stores. His two idols, he once remarked, were LBJ, who terrorized his opponents without pity, and FDR, who had the gift of charming the opposition into submission, unaware they were being shafted.

Your leverage is minimal, of course, if you're easily replaced, like the drone with no more than a high-sounding title. But suppose you have a specialized knowledge of the duties involved in your job. Or better still, suppose you know a little too much about some of your company's marginal activities—not necessarily illegal, but in the grey area. Then your sought-after stratagem has some clout.

A corporation, fearful of an antitrust suit, sought a divestiture of some of its subsidiaries. Competitors watched closely to assure the legitimacy of each move. The line between illusion and reality in the divestiture grew blurred as the company sought to avoid violations of the guidelines set out by the Justice Department. It relied a great deal—too much—upon the expertise of one of its executive vice-presidents. He demanded, and received, a substantial salary increase and sizable stock bonus—not because he was irreplaceable, but simply because the company learned, too late, that he was a hot property in the corporate jungle, not above selling what he knew for a bigger job and higher salary.

> The Persian Picaroon, with his morals sitting easy about him, a rogue indeed, but not a malicious one, with as much wit and cunning as enable him to dupe others, and as much vanity as to afford them perpetual means of retaliation.[5]
> ——————————————— *Heroes and Heroines of Fiction.*

What Price Knavery   It's an American myth that no man who can make millions and rise to the top of a corporation can still be an idiot in his human relationships. But he can—and you don't have to be a Peter Drucker in management analysis to find examples. The higher some executives rise in the corporate structure, and the more they are laden with honors, the more they lose contact with reality and the less resistant they become to the deceptions of predators around and below them.

The mayhems range from the subtle, worthy of a career diplomat, to the brutal and humiliating, one no less blood-letting than the other.

Hardly possible, you will say. Much too glib an assumption. You may be right. Still, the last statement was made by the head of a large management consulting firm. And what preceded is a consensus of opinion among many climbers of the pyramid, middle and top level, gathered during the writing of this book. It reflects experiences in a wide variety of corporate enterprises, large and small.

Before you decide that the executive immediately ahead of you is an obstacle that must be sidetracked or dethroned, one way or another, ask yourself: What are his roots in the organization, how deep do they run and how strong? Your harpoon could turn into a boomerang.

And don't count on the loyalty of your co-workers in trying to dislodge an immediate superior who is obnoxious or woefully incompetent. They may shed a tear or two with you after each encounter, but in a showdown, it's every man for himself. If your exposure results in a demotion or discharge, you've suddenly become someone to be avoided. Co-workers will instinctively turn away, as if your bad luck might rub off. Deception ill fits the capo when it threatens the head of the family; he is doomed as soon as the finger of suspicion points in his direction.

Your manipulative efforts will prove more rewarding if you make a serious effort to evaluate the strengths and weaknesses of The Big One. Don't let the image of the oversized desk with its long row of pushbuttons and the corner carpeted office obscure the fact that he too lives precariously. It's sound strategy to weigh his shortfalls in shaping your maneuvers—never, of course, giving the slightest sign of your quest. You are ever obsequious. This is no easy task. It's never easy to kiss the hand you'd like to cut off.

A few executives—pitifully few—are like Silly Putty in reacting to rebellious subordinates. They absorb the small insults, the needling of pride and mangling of ego, sometimes even questioning their own judgment. "Maybe they have a point!" But most are like rock. A hard blow, or series of small ones, and they break—or try to break—those arrayed against them, even though instinctively aware that these convulsive efforts do no more than accelerate their own downfall.

Status terms like President, Vice-President, or Chief Executive, are fluid in today's corporate hierarchies. Duties overlap. Powers merge. But behind this imprecision, in every division or department, there is a No. 1 to whom others must answer.

My observations, based on dealings with corporate executives for many years, in and out of litigation, suggest the following basic types.

1. The insecure, defensive-minded manager, suspicious of his subordinates, quick to assert his authority, easily provoked to demote, transfer, or limit the prerogatives of anyone who is suggested to him as posing even a remote threat to his position. He is basically a fearful man, obsessed with security more than success. Submissive to whatever the company decrees, he is content to share even vicariously in the glory of its achievements.

2. The easy-going, mild-mannered executive of average ability, not overbright, loath to believe that one of his flock would conspire against, or deceive, him. A vanishing breed in today's managerial community; the type who adorns the walls of his office with such gems of sophistication as "The best way to make money is to stop losing it." No subordinate objects that he doesn't listen, the trouble is he listens to everyone, and like Jimmy Carter, can't arrive at a firm decision, one that won't be different tomorrow from what it is today.

Easiest to manipulate in this category is the executive, newly hired or elevated from the ranks and driven by a desire to "be one of the boys," "liked by all." Until he discovers that what counts is production and discipline, and that to be respected is good, but to be feared is better, he is a ripe target for whatever manipulation you have in mind.

But a word of caution is in order.

I heard a recently promoted executive remark: "The bastards simply took advantage of my trust in them. Now I don't give a damn what they think of me. They toe the line and meet production schedules or else."

Neatly said, but when he created a reign of terror, the results were catastrophic. He swung too far, too fast. Loving or hating are not good management tools. An executive should never forget that his subordinates depend on him for their job, and that dependence breeds suspicion and fear—as it should, to a measure. Ideally, he should stimulate them to better performance in their *own* interest, not because they fear or love their superior.

3. The dynamic, success-oriented No. 1, preoccupied with

setting and meeting new goals and establishing himself as
The Man, who endows his orders with the sanctity of an
edict of the College of Cardinals. His gnat-size conscience
is never a bar to firing a loyal or productive subordinate, if
it will enhance his own image or protect his rear. This is the
prototype most likely to appear on the front cover of *Forbes*
or *Business Week*.

He is driven by the idolatry of his own talents and
hunger for their recognition. He tolerates mediocrity in
his subordinates for two reasons: it is usually too pervasive
to uproot summarily and he feels more secure in the
contrast it offers. His peers in the corporate world are
regarded with suspicion; if they threaten his domain, they
are enemies to be destroyed. Maccoby put it neatly in *The
Gamesman*: the jungle fighters are either lions or foxes;
lions are conquerors who build empires if they are
successful, while foxes move ahead from their nests by
stealth and deception.

4. The mediocre or incompetent, thrust into responsibilities
   over his head, leaning heavily on his staff in making
   decisions, on even the most mundane matters; receptive to
   suggestions, but never sure which to accept or reject;
   pretentious, holding tight to the perks of his office.

5. The giant now grown tired and indecisive, in his middle or
   late sixties, perhaps showing signs of senility, with only
   occasional flashes of the brilliance that made him No. 1, yet
   reluctant to leave the trappings of the throne. Only dimly
   does he sense his plight of lapsed yesterdays and
   foreclosed tomorrows. Most of such relics deserve the
   mayhem they eventually receive.

Talents they once possessed for decision making have become
atrophied by age, paranoia, recurrent bouts of depression, or
withdrawals from the realities of the corporate world around
them. Now no more than fading symbols of power and rank, they
block many paths to promotion, like a well-entrenched log dam-
ming a swift current. A good example was Sewell Avery of
Montgomery Ward, whose name was shortened by his executives
to one word: "Slavery." With something less than good reason, he
fired or forced the resignation of over sixty first vice-presidents
during his reign. A beautiful candidate for a rape.

I know one top executive who, in his dotage, developed a

new technique of administration. Instead of delegating by jobs to be done or duties to be performed, he began to delegate by specific results. Quotas were pinpointed and widely posted. "Your department is tagged for 30,000 units monthly" or "I want $350,000 gross sales each month from your territory." His demands were unrealistic, impossible. As one subordinate remarked to me: "We would have been satisfied with crude measurements, not a fixed requirement that he would call us to task for, if not met to the letter. So we screwed him, in a dozen ways, like predating shipments and doctoring invoices. He didn't last long."

Now for a few basic caveats in planning your maneuvers to dethrone No. 1. Remember at the outset that your prime loyalty is not to the organization, but to the man you seek to depose. Each move you make must subtly reflect this feeling. The aged Emperor Franz Josef of Austria-Hungary was said to have remarked, when a minister was suggested for promotion because he was a patriot: "Yes, but is he a patriot for *me*?"[6]

No less important: Create no crisis or situation requiring major decisions. No bad mouthing. Conform. Agree. Merge into the whole. No precipitous moves until you have made a careful evaluation of the risks involved. Weigh each alternative as if your business life depended on it—because it does.

Balance risks against gains. And match strategy to need. It's senseless to use a blunderbuss when a gentle shove will do. I have seen executives drawn into a common effort by the ineptitude of their superior, reacting to his inability to act effectively. They simply built a wall around him, discharging his functions except for the required amenities, just as if he were not there. His uselessness gradually emerged, levelling the image of master. Pride dies hard, but it does die, eventually. And few executives survive the loss. Never overlook this maneuver, particularly if you can join others as co-conspirators.

Consider next the deceptions of *over-response* and *delayed response*. Given an assignment, respond with unusual dispatch, with such overwhelming data and minutiae that the master is suddenly thrust into a defensive posture, forced to make decisions he is unprepared to make. He may forego any decision at all, respond impulsively, or scrap the entire project. In any event, you have exposed areas of vulnerability that might otherwise have remained hidden. The *over-response* maneuver is particularly suited to type 3.

You'll have no trouble identifying him. He's Captain Queeg of *The Caine Mutiny,* who fumed about who pilfered the quart of berries while war raged all around him. His control procedures are so tight that compliance becomes more important than the objective they seek to accomplish.

The more the object of your knavery resembles Captain Queeg, the clearer becomes your strategy. Over-comply with each regulation, form, and directive, even to the point of defeating common sense. You create a creeping bureaucracy, blindly enamoured of the directives of The Big One. Carried far enough, the department can become as rudderless as the ship of Captain Queeg.

Consider the accelerating stratagem of one subordinate in a Midwest food processing plant. "This new production head wanted strict compliance with each regulation, some were pure hogwash. So I gave it to him. In spades, doubled. I took his directives and made them up into a manual for department heads. It was a thick book of minute orders and guidelines, from acceptable periods in the john to cleaning and placement of each tool at the end of the day's work. Voluminous. Authoritative. He liked it with a reverence. It was his passport to immortality in the corporate structure. After a few weeks it made him look like the straightlaced son of a bitch that he was. In six months they shipped him East to Personnel."

It is important to remember, however, that the status-ridden chief, who climbed many weary miles to reach his present position, is not likely to carelessly expose his flanks. The shrewdness that drove him before will propel him now. He may still envision himself as a Gulliver encircled by an army of Lilliputians.

Try the delayed report maneuver with the aged, worn-out No. 1. By the time you submit the report, he may have forgotten the assignment he gave you, may bury it in the mountain of papers cluttering his desk, or, more likely, lose interest in the project.

A small crack, to be sure, but repeated often enough and spread around in the right quarters, it could begin the erosion of the Emperor's image. Not everybody repeats rumors and gossip.

Most improve on them. Now suppose the roles are reversed, and No. 1 is the raper and one of his subordinates the rapee. You are the head of a division and anxious to ease out an aging, forgetful executive under your command, who is no less determined to await the mandatory retirement age. Subtle reminders pass unheeded. You have no taste for execution by indirection as by curtailing his authority, moving his corner office to a cubbyhole near the Men's Room, or changing his title. Too obvious. Too patently cruel.

To meet this situation, you adopt a more subtle but no less effective stratagem. You suborn one or two junior executives anxious to move closer to the throne, making them your surrogates in the humiliation of their older colleague. Behind a façade of deference to rank, they will belittle his proposals or comments at staff meetings, gradually eroding his image.

Under your guidance, the criticisms will gradually grow more barbed with each meeting, yet never mount to an open confrontation. Since retaliation is only possible against an equal, the play becomes a one-sided contest, with the end never in doubt. After this maneuver, you may feel as if you need debriefing before you re-enter the human race.

Certainly a dastardly manipulation, worthy only of someone with the morals of Machiavelli or the cunning of Richard Nixon. But let me repeat what I expressed earlier: corporate integrity is a phrase that should be divorced on the grounds of incompatibility.

Knavery takes many forms in the corporate ranks, from the subtle to the brazen. A well-known figure in the entertainment industry was described to me by one of his former associates:

"The man seems incapable of guile or deceit. He projects sincerity, concern for your pride and well being, indifference to the customary symbols of power. Yet he is at heart a conniving bastard, who buried a half-dozen rivals for his present post, by forced resignation or transfer to a lesser job. Get too smart and your head rolls. The funny part of it is that not one of them—myself included—was aware of the knife until they were actually skewered. Even more amazing is how often he left his victims with the feelings they were not actually knifed, or if the blood-letting was too obvious to be overlooked, that he was genuinely sorry for what happened."

Weakness Is Never Beautiful, But It Sometimes Helps

> God hath chosen the weak things of the world to confound the things that are mighty.
> ───────────────────────────────── St. Paul

Weakness is not only traditionally unproductive, but it evokes little sympathy in the corridors of business or politics. We feel safer, more comfortable, with the "tough guy," adept in eyeball-to-eyeball confrontation and devious manipulation, as typified by Kissinger, and by Nixon in his balmier days. But a façade of weakness can, in some instances, be a powerful tool of deception for the business executive.

Whenever a problem arises that involves an interplay of personalities, study carefully the possible use of this maneuver. There is a deceptive strength in a planned show of weakness. It can be manipulated to an innocuous put-down of another, or an inducement to his acceptance of something you want him to accept but dare not offer directly.

Take the sports promotor I know who is a positive genius at projecting an image of utter fatigue when trying to close a difficult deal. His speech and mannerisms convey the message, loud and clear. "Oh, what the hell. Do I have to go all over this again? Can't you take my word for it?"

His words trail off in a weary lament. Such deceptions tend to put the listener on the defensive, giving him a sense of guilt in pressing his point.

Weakness is obviously a one-time maneuver. A long-term posture would turn you into a doormat, with footprints down the length of your back. To insolence, jealousy, or aggression, or to a predator, weakness breeds contempt, and unless this is the reaction you are inviting for your own tactical advantage, forget the humble pie.

If you elect to try this ploy of deception, note that the image of weakness, fragile at best, should not be sustained any longer than necessary, lest it become transparent. Once the deceivee has become aware of the deceiver's put-on, further approaches are wisely abandoned. Forgiveness is a fickle emotion, too shifting to be relied upon.

John Brent (a pseudonym for the personnel manager of a large conglomerate, charged with hiring, firing, and salary manipulations) played the role of harried executive to full advantage. He confronted an employee who he decided was ill-suited to his job and overpaid.

"I'm sorry as hell, Bill, but I've got an order to transfer you to inventory control. It's a lousy break. I know how well you have handled your present job—the reports have all been good. Why they want to demote a man like you is beyond me. I've given up trying to make rhyme or reason for some of their decisions. And that worries me plenty." Incidentally, "discharged" is rarely used today. It's "terminal separation," "relocation recommendation," or "executive relocation."

At this point, John shakes his head, puts on a freeze-dry smile and shrugs his shoulders in a gesture of helplessness.

"But what the hell can I do? Believe me, Bill, this job is strictly for the birds." He would have ruined it all by saying: "I know it will be hard as hell to get along without you, but starting Monday, we're going to try hard, awfully hard."

He watches the other carefully. He has decided to reduce the salary cut involved in the transfer, but only if he senses that Bill may resign—something he does not want to happen at this point.

Weakness and humiliation have inspired a sympathy of sorts for the personnel manager. They made him a victim of the system instead of a part of it. A show of power and authority would have linked him to the "they" that ordered the demotion and salary cut. He now appeared as no more than a surrogate in carrying out the company decision, an almost equal-in-rank figure to the employee facing him. Self-deprecation was a small price to pay for the success of this put-on.

John Brent knows that denying power or authority gives him a powerful weapon in negotiating contracts or compromising labor disputes. If he can successfully project this put-on, he has divorced himself from a rapacious company, the power clique hungry for the best possible deal.

One executive I know was "terminally separated" on Friday, with all the amenities suitable to the occasion, but appeared at the office the following Monday.

"Sorry, Bill," he was told, "but what we intended to say was 'You're terminated. Discharged.'"

"I know," the other nodded. "I thought it over during the weekend, and decided to stay on for another year, maybe longer. It would be good for both of us. You see, I know a little too much about some of our questionable trade practices, and if I went to a competitor and talked—" He shrugged his shoulders. "Well, you know how it is. Besides I need the money. I really do."

He stayed on—until retirement age.

The role of weakness is played at the expense of machismo, hence is not too popular a put-on. Success is equated with toughness, firmness, unequivocal decisions. But a carefully staged show of weakness, short of utter stupidity, can pay off handsomely.

> *Manager:* What happened to the Acme order? It was due for shipment last week.
> *You:* It went out last night.
> *Manager:* Last night! What the hell's going on in your department? That's the third delayed shipment in a month.
> *You:* I know, I know. I'm working ten hours a day to clear up the backlog. One night I even slept at the plant, too tired to drive home.[Call for a glass of water and then pop two aspirin.] There's just so much the body can take. God knows, I'm trying hard.
> *Manager:* Well, damn it, try harder.
> *You:* (after a long sigh): Will do. I've been going around in a half-stupor from overwork. Look at the rings under these eyes. There's not a man in my department hasn't worked just as hard.[Actually they barely get up a sweat.] I can't drive them much harder. But I'll try.[Another long sigh and wipe of the brow.] Believe me, I'll try."

I know fairly well a retired corporate executive who, quite by accident, became a crack labor negotiator with a remarkable track record in fitting union demands to company offers. His office was Spartan in its simplicity: a battered desk and three straight-backed chairs, with a single file cabinet. The walls were bare, although he could have covered all four of them with diplomas, plaques, testimonials, and photographs showing him hobnobbing with national figures. His put-on with labor was a sympathy for the rationale of their demands, and bitterness at the intransigence of the employer. With the company he used the same put-on in reverse. He was so well adjusted to the environment that sometimes you couldn't tell which was the environment and which was the man.

He managed to impart an impression of bone-deep weariness and fatigue in his negotiations, as if he was at the tail end of his endurance. He drew your sympathy. You felt he deserved better for his efforts, that he was possibly not the strongest mediator but that for *you,* he was the best.

And that, my good friend, is how you can make even weakness look beautiful.

Overworked and Indispensable

> Of all areas of human contact, there is none where first appearances are more deceiving than in the corporate hierarchy.

Whether for real, or a put-on, every corporate structure has its share of them: the middle-rung executive, so obviously overworked and exhausted that he tells you in a single glance, "I can't take much more of this." The role is not too difficult to play. Your objective, of course, is the illusion of indispensability and super-devotion to your job. When you attend a staff meeting or conference toward the end of the day, or report to your superior, it is always with that tired look, as if you have reached the outer limit of your endurance. Lean back in your chair, loosen your tie, take off your glasses, and massage the bridge of your nose, wearing an expression that says unmistakably: "How much more can a human body take?"

Try being the first to arrive in the morning and the last to leave, always with a bulging briefcase, hinting of unfinished work to be done at home.

Working long hours could be the first sign of an embezzlement in the making, or an over-identification with the company. But it does make for increased exposure, and could be an effective put-on for promotion. This gambit is particularly effective when your upward climb is stalled by a "blocker," a term used in corporate circles to designate an executive who knows he is not going anywhere and is determined that you don't move ahead of him. But remember: increased visibility is only helpful in overcoming "blockage," or making you appear indispensable, if the right people see it.

And above all, do not delude yourself into thinking that consistent loyalty to your corporate employer is anything more than a commodity you are selling. It does not make you irreplaceable. Forget the notion that long hours and years of solid service guarantee success, security, or promotion, or even help you keep your job. You are expendable—more than you think. That's the way it always was and always will be.

Moreover, in this crazy world of twisted values, don't expect that your bright ideas for improving the corporate welfare will make you indispensable. If they're accepted by your superior, you run the risk of building yourself into a threat to his superiority. If they're rejected, it could be just as bad. People don't forgive a man whose good advice they once turned down, any more than they forgive someone they once wronged.

Indispensability is, of course, an illusion. The trick is to buttress that illusion, using whatever artifices the situation suggests or the circumstances make possible. The insecure executive, fearful of encroachments on his power base, will be ever alert for whatever feeds his mirage, no matter how trivial. He will, for example, always find something to change in whatever a subordinate hands him, no matter how small. He will give it more than the appearance of a finishing touch. The change or addition must look important, something for which he displays a unique capability. And if it's a suggestion for a new procedure or an improvement in an existing practice, he'll find something, *anything* to add, so that it becomes a joint contribution.

A less subtle put-on is the cluttered desk. A clean surface, bare as a billiard ball, except for neatly arranged work material along one edge, is for the top executive who has reached his niche and has no superior to impress. A desk littered with reports, correspondence, and the minutiae of the daily routine, speaks of a workhorse, dedicated to his job. It helps if you have a disarray of books on an end table near your desk, with titles relating to your present job or the one you aspire to. Slip pieces of paper in the volumes as markers, and be sure the titles are visible.

A good put-on will show just enough clutter to suggest you're a dedicated drone, buried deep in your work, but not enough to give the impression you're a slob. A few charts on the wall are helpful. They can relate to any phase of your work, even if copied from a trade magazine or manual, with your own figures and legends filled in.

But this maneuver can be overplayed and become a transparent gesture. I hired a young lawyer anxious to impress me and my two partners with his industry, hinting of the kind of indispensability that makes for an eventual junior partnership. His desk and the table adjoining it were piled high with a variety of legal texts and law periodicals, each with numerous markers. This was a man obviously steeped deep in his work. An impressive tableau, but too rigged.

When I thumbed through this material in his absence, and read the pages with markers, I saw that they had no relevance whatever to the cases assigned to him. They presented no consistent pattern of interest.

"What are you working on with all this material?" I later asked him. For a moment he stared, groping for an appropriate answer, like a paramour caught *in flagrante delicto*. He mumbled some reply, but the put-on became a put-down. The props soon disappeared.

Making What You Have to Do Look Like What You Want to Do   A ploy occasionally used to mask weakness or mediocrity is to make what you are forced to do look like what you wanted or decided to do. Machiavelli put it neatly:

"Prudent men make the best of circumstances in their actions and, although constrained by necessity to a certain course, make it appear as if done from their own liberality."

If, for example, you are compelled against your wishes to a course of action that will be regarded as good by your subordinates, then at least make it appear that the happening is because of your own magnanimity. The president of a large university announced to the department heads at a conference that he wanted more time devoted to original research, and to this end favored a 10% reduction in class hours for associate and full professors. A department head that I knew, sorely tried by the lackadaisical attitude of some of his staff and the hostility of a few, beat the gun by announcing to them the imminent approval "of something I've long worked for."

If you know the minimum wage in your business will soon rise to $4.00 an hour, it's a good move to "voluntarily" increase the wages of your employees to that level. Conversely, if you are in the unenviable position of being compelled to do something that is unpopular, look for likely prospects to take the credit. Firing an employee who is popular with co-workers, for example, is a sticky task, best shifted, wherever possible, to a subordinate. Like the primitive tribesmen who cut off the head of the bearer of bad news, we still instinctively attribute something of the authorship of such news to the one telling us about it.

Puts-Ons at Meetings or Staff Conferences

> The trail of the serpent reaches into all the lucrative professions and practices of man. Each has its own wrongs. Each finds a tender and very intelligent conscience a disqualification for success. Each requires of the practitioner a certain shutting of the eyes, a certain dapperness and compliance, an acceptance of customs.[7]
> — *Emerson*

Meetings or staff conferences are either a big yawn or a close encounter of the worst kind, depending on the executive presiding. It has been my observation, in researching hierarchical manipulations, that the higher the level of personnel at staff meetings, the more devious are the devices employed: by No. 1 to enhance his posture, get approval of measures he's already marked for approval, cut down to size an over-achiever or smart-ass subordinate, or enhance the status of a favored deputy; and by No. 2, the subordinate, to display his abilities or hide his shortcomings.

The scope of put-ons you can practice at staff conferences or meetings depends on where you sit. If you are at the head of the table, your maneuvers will obviously be different from those of your acolytes.

Whatever your status, you can profit from some of the maneuvers I encountered. If you are starry-eyed, steeped deep in Billy Graham religiosity, skip this section.

Maneuvers of the Master   Adopt a fixed schedule for regular meetings, and, wherever possible, an agenda of the major subjects to be discussed; for example, "Management options regarding the possible impact of a price increase," "Measures we can take now to avoid layoffs if a recession develops," or "How to smooth out the cyclical nature of the market for our products." Not to receive definitive solutions to any part of these problems, but to sustain the image of importance. Timing plays a major role. It invests the conferences with a ritualistic significance.

"What actually takes place is usually fluffed up to look important," the division head of a medium-sized plant told me, "and the decisions reached are generally those I already made, either alone or in conjunction with headquarters, but I manage to let the staff feel they're their own. It's not too difficult if you know your staff and how to steer the discussion."

As the chief, you should not reveal too much of yourself, your likes and dislikes, or your fears and uncertainties. Strategically, this places you in a more maneuverable position. You can more readily control dissidents or strengthen a view you favor. Your moves are less suspect, less predictable. You can contribute to the discussion liberally, even impressively, yet communicate little of yourself and nothing of what you have in mind. Try talking without communicating. It's not too difficult.

Let's assume your subordinates are, for the most part, not too expressive. You know the meeting needs an infusion of give and take to confer a semblance of importance. After all, the object is to create the illusion of employee participation in major decisions, a sense of being included in the power structure.

And what a heady feeling it is—how they revel in the comradeship and the dizzying sensation of being a part of the inner circle! So you designate and brief two or three who will lead the discussion on specific subjects. Select participants who are leaders, not sheep; the articulate, not the muted who wouldn't know how to lead a moment of silent prayer.

The more diverse the group, the better. Rivals for your favor or promotion are likely to balance out each other and prevent what you fear most: unanimity of opinion contrary to something you've already decided.

Now let us suppose you are opposed to changes proposed by some of your managers and likely to win approval at the next staff meeting. Make a friendly subordinate your surrogate to handle the opposition, using some of your own sidetracking devices:

"I think we're overlooking a few basic fallacies in this plan. . . ."

"We simply can't rush into this project; it needs more planning . . ."

"I've given a lot of thought to this proposal. It's not all white or black. Here are some of the greys that deserve consideration."

Brief him on the maneuvers to contain the proponents, while you maintain a steady hand and a Buddha inscrutability. The throne remains impartial. Use the same manipulation to cut down to size one of your subordinates who is too upbeat, moving too fast and posing a future threat to your security. I recommend the strategy of one executive, as described by one of his subordinates:

"His technique for cutting down the opposition was simplicity itself and something wondrous to behold. He was like Muhammad Ali at his best. He knew instinctively when to lie back, noncommittal, when to dance around the arguments of intended victims, stating and restating them until fixed firmly in his sights, then moving in for the kill—cool, quick, and clean."

Assume, however, you lack a suitable delegate and must play the dual role of impartial chairman and devil's advocate. Three basic stratagems are available: *confuse, browbeat,* and *divert.* Their effectiveness depends upon your manipulative ability. It can range from the Kissinger adroitness to the bone-crushing pressure of Lyndon Johnson, but whatever your talent for deception, the manipulations must be carefully planned.

Mr. Confuse will come prepared with an impressive assortment of charts with columns of equations, drawings, and statistical data. Figures are quoted, charts displayed on racks or by passing them around. Copies of reports or his recommendations are distributed. Bewildering. Impressive. As persuasive as the recommendations of the President's Council of Economic Advisors, and as intelligible.

"You can see, gentlemen, the basic trend is in the direction opposite to where this proposal will take us."

Who among those assembled will question the conclusions flowing from such herculean efforts?

Mr. Browbeat uses the bludgeon of impatience and incredulity. "Look at this proposal carefully and you can't help seeing it's regressive. Instead of stimulating sales, it will lower them. To say nothing of what it will do to the good will of our customers. I can't see how anyone who has studied this problem, even superficially, can reach any other conclusion." You shake your head in disbelief at such a possibility. "All right, now let's get on to the next subject."

"Mr. Chairman, there's a thought that comes to mind."

At this point, you've developed a slight hearing impairment and so move right on.

Mr. Divert will, in the best tradition of the diversionary ploy (see Chapter 6), switch attention from the main thrust of the proposal. His objective is time and more time, delay and more delay. So he selects for discussion something that looks married to the principal thesis, but is actually light-years away.

"Extending our product line at this time raises serious questions of feasibility. [Actually the proposal relates to product improvement.] We should make an in-depth study of the cost factor involved. That could be a barrier. Look what happened a few months ago on the cost overrun in Tom Jones' project. [Actually a different concept.] Let's put this over for a few weeks until I can come up with some facts and figures."

So you bury the projected plan in a sea of contentions about the wisdom of increasing production costs at this crucial period. If a participant veers away from the distraction, as chairman you lace your responses with qualifiers and exit clauses to protect you against an unraveling of the diversion.

Deceptions of the Acolyte

A man who knows the ways of the Court is master of his gestures, his eyes and his face; he is deep, impenetrable;

he pretends not to notice injuries done him, he smiles to his
enemies, controls his temper, disguises his passions, be-
lies his heart, speaks and acts against his real opinions. All
this elaborate procedure is merely a device which we call
deceitfulness.

———————————————— *Jean de La Bruyere, Characters.*

To the neophyte, reluctant to set his sails until he sees the direction of the wind, a holding pattern is in order. Be visible, but not
too visible. Tread water, stirring no waves, not even a ripple. Your
objective is maximum likeability, steering a middle course, contributing additions or clarifications, never contradictions, moving
always from the specific to the general. The image you covet is
"agreeable," "clearheaded." This is not acquired by small
triumphs at the expense of others. I have sat in at enough of these
meetings to observe how quickly some fledgling executives learn
the Delphic art of talking without communicating. They drop no
pearls of wisdom, expose no fallacies, create no conflicts.

But their put-ons—so pleasant to the ear, and so much
garbage to the mind—pave the way upward.

It's good strategy rarely to speak first on a subject likely to
be controversial, even if you're bursting to explode with a gem of
a contribution. Let the others vent their ideas, and pay particular
attention to the views of your superior. No less important than
put-ons to mask incompetence or mediocrity are those maneuvers aimed at concealing cleverness at a meeting or conference,
particularly where you would be likely to ruffle the feathers of
your superiors or equals, and stamp you in their eyes as an
over-bright hard-ass, to be carefully watched in the future.

I suggest you memorize a few passages from the *Dictionary
of Contemporary Quotations, The Home Book of Bible Quotations,* and
Bartlett's Familiar Quotations. Select quotes so general they can
apply to almost any situation that may arise. At the appropriate
moment, when you're not sure what view to express and you've
simply *got* to say something, drop your pearl. Even if its only
remotely relevant, the chances are that no one will know the
difference. Your maneuver may serve to hide the void that passes
for understanding, masking it under a put-on of profundity.

To experienced hands, who know that hard decisions on
major matters are rarely made at these conferences, the games

played are jockeying for recognition, riding on the ideas of others, or cutting them down, as gently and unobtrusively as possible. The general idea is to do to him, what he'd like to do to you, but to do it first. Will Rogers put it neatly: "Trickery is what the other fellow does to you, never what you do to him."

And when the conference is all over, and your superior— or whoever puts the question to you—asks what was accomplished at the meeting, drop the familiar sugar plum: "A great conference! The problems were really clarified. No question about it. We can see them more clearly now. And the way all points of view were developed—just great!"

Let's suppose you know the meeting will discuss some of the shortcomings in your department. As manager, you will be called upon for explanation. It's good strategy to avoid meeting the issue head-on. Look for euphemisms and word covers to soften the impact of your mistakes or errors in judgment. A catastrophic blunder is never described in terms of a major disaster, but as "a shortfall resulting from factors not to be anticipated" or "the cumulative result of variables beyond our control."

An honest statement might raise questions about your competency, and prove embarrassing in the presence of the Chief Executive and your equals. And if you're caught in a practice not wholly within the parameters of corporate morality, you simply acted to "contain a situation that required containment."

Language today, in the corporate as well as public sectors, is so euphemized that meanings become lost in a jungle of double-speak. With a little practice, you can manipulate words to transmute accountability into nonaccountability, and with a more sharpened skill, even arrange your language to create two contradictory beliefs simultaneously. George Orwell gave a memorable example in his novel *1984,* in describing the lettering on the entrance to the Ministry of Truth:

> War Is Peace
> Freedom Is Slavery
> Ignorance Is Strength

A Sensible Risk—Never a Foolish Error   The exculpatory maneuver can either polish the halo you wear or bury it. It depends on how adept you are in distinguishing between an excuse and an explanation. To a corporate executive, it's almost a necessity—the ability to palliate a grievous error in judgment.

A division head paid the supreme accolade to one of his managers: "That man could fall into a pit of horseshit up to his eyeballs and come out smelling like a rose. He's that kind of a sweet talker."

Here are a few maneuvers that may give you some insight into how to make a foolish error look like a brave or sensible risk.

1. Maximize your motive, while minimizing the predictability of what happened.
2. Look for sharing partners in the decision making, or in its execution—those who perhaps unknowingly contributed to the debacle, even if their contribution is minor. Shared responsibility does something to your image. Top management is likely to feel that if several other managers thought as you did, your decision could not have been so ill advised after all.
3. Blow up the possible rewards in the failed project, while minimizing the risks, if any, that were apparent at that time.
4. Look for possible adverse effects if the project had been delayed or scrapped. Your credibility is the key here. Calamitous consequences can be ascribed to the do-nothing decision. Point to Gillette's gamble that the stainless steel blade would, like so many shaving gimmicks, just fade away. No less disastrous, you can convincingly argue, was the decision of Detroit car manufacturers that small-sized imports were a fad that would soon pass.
5. Stress the non-avoidability of the risks undertaken. "I know that good management doesn't like to take major risks, so it avoids them. But some risks are thrust upon us, and just can't be swept under the rug. This was one of them. Actually, gentlemen, there was no alternative to the decision I made." A good fail-safe maneuver.

Marrying risk to probability requires good judgment, not the sweep of enthusiasm. The trick is to make your disaster look like something born out of both. Management worships the bullishness of youth, its creativity and drive for new directions in matching techniques and products to market needs. But it is no less admiring of the reasoned judgment that proceeds at pedestrian pace.

4. Lawyer Put-Ons

I cannot tell you, sir, who he is, and I would be loth to speak ill of any person who I do not know deserves it, but I am afraid he is an attorney.

——————————————————————— *Samuel Johnson*

The Doctored Image   Lawyers are particularly adept in the deceptions and bluffs that shape a winning image. I know most attorneys will grow apoplectic at the thought they are pretenders, in so much of their professional and social conduct, in the mannerisms, dress, speech, or quirks they have affected over the years.

The game rules allow for an infinite variety of deceptions: whatever catches the eye, arrests attention, or lifts one out of the swarm of practitioners is permissible. Ability is a basic ingredient, to be sure, but it need be no more than average. In possibly no other profession do stratagems of deception and bluff reap bigger dividends, or more effectively hide mediocrity.

There is much you can learn from these manipulations.

Legal upmanship is a fascinating study in human nature, and a fitting chapter in the story of Machiavellian arts. Let me describe some of the gambits I have observed—and no doubt used myself in one form or another—in a long career at the bar. Whatever your field of activity, you will find some of these ploys helpful.

Lawyer put-ons are as varied as they are ingenious. They won't turn a clod into a national celebrity, or put him on the Today Show to pontificate on what's wrong with the legal profession, but given average talent and a fair amount of *chutzpah,* he can acquire an image of sorts.

> "Virtue is now in the middle," said the Devil as he sat down between two lawyers.
> ———————————————— *Swedish Proverb*

I heard a criminal lawyer of some renown talking to a small group of young lawyers over cocktails, after his lecture which was little more than an ego trip.

"You've got to build an image that stands out. Look for the right cases to try, not the kind you know are likely to be reported in the back pages of your local newspaper below the shipping news or the recipes. When they show up, take them to trial. Don't take a plea. And when you get an acquittal, don't wait for the press to come to you. Go to them, with a newsworthy twist or two to your story. And be sure your name is spelled right."

A little later, he dropped this nugget of advice: "Ready identification is important, not only in your profession, but in any calling, even if it's only a façade. You create it out of an infinite number of small deceptions and bluffs. For example, I would suggest you look for areas of disagreement in community affairs and social issues, about which to express your views, the more volatile the better. A lawyer should be heard *in* court and *out* of court.

And don't parrot the familiar. Strike a fresh and arresting note in what you say. If you walk into a room and discover that everyone is in agreement on some subject, think up a contrary view, the more outrageous the better. You are not looking for popular support, only recognition—even though to some you'll be a real bastard for the stand you've taken."

Your bluff and huff can range from the subtle to the outlandish, one no less productive of an arresting image than the other. What will pass as chic for one will be *schlock* for another. Percy Foreman, for example, the legendary Texas criminal lawyer, used as the return address on his envelopes "Percy 77002," thereby establishing beyond dispute the range and depth of his fame. Colorful. Audacious. To Louis Nizer or F. Lee Bailey, it would be strictly bush league.

Social put-ons are always helpful. Your image as an upcoming lawyer or business executive is enhanced, for example, if you cultivate a distinctive avocation, like collecting African art or Sixth Century Gregorian chants. Learn well the shop talk of your interest, so you can pass as an expert, even if your knowledge is skin-deep. Short vacations at watering holes like Biarritz, Majorca, or Caneel Bay contribute to the image.

Earl Rogers, the courtroom giant of a few generations ago, had his famous lorgnette, with a golden handle and black ribbon. It seemed a natural part of his thin face with its ascetic features. On any other trial lawyer of his day—or in our time—it would be an affectation. Rogers waved it like a magic wand, pointing and gesturing, occasionally lifting it to peer intently at a witness during cross-examination, as if in disbelief that he could utter so profound a falsehood. A newspaper cartoon, showing only a lorgnette, was entitled "King of the Courtroom." No one could doubt who it described.

> A lie, turned topsy-turvy, can be prinked and tinselled out, decked in plumage new and fine, till none knows its lean old carcass.[1]
>
> ———————————————————— *Henrik Ibsen*

To manipulate the ordinary so it looks extraordinary, is the highest form of deception. It is a common practice, for example, for lawyers who win a jury verdict or sizeable settlement in a personal injury action to minimize the injuries in the account they give to the press. The verdict looms proportionately higher, and so does their reputation for being able to get much for little. Fifty thousand dollars sounds small for several fractured vertebrae, but is impressively high for bruises and contusions.

The physical aspects of a put-on are as important to the attorney as to any other craftsman. The walls of my first office were lined floor to ceiling with impressive-looking law digests and textbooks that were no more than cardboard facings resembling bound volumes; the legal files piled high on the desk were discards from my neighbor next door. The accouterments spoke of a busy and successful young lawyer, when, in fact, I found it necessary to work a short shift as doorman at the old Paramount Theatre in New York to help pay my expenses.

Whatever your business or profession, you can profit from observing how quickly young lawyers learn the unwritten rules for using small deceptions to create a desired image. These maneuvers they learn from their peers and the small talk at conventions and social gatherings of their colleagues. They are nowhere to be found in law books, law school courses, or popular guides on how to succeed in your profession or business. The gambits try to embellish the ordinary with the magic of something extraordinary, whether describing the last trial or the appeal or motion argued, all of which were won, unexpectedly and undeservedly.

To veterans at the bar, some of these put-ons are sickly transparent, reminiscent of fledgling actors jockeying for recognition at try-outs for a new production. But to the upcoming they feed an ego hungry for recognition, no matter how small the crumbs. Besides, there is a therapeutic effect in giving life to a doctored image. As one character remarked: "After a few Manhattans and some heady stories, I become F. Lee Bailey at his best. I soar up and up, like a kite torn from its string."

A few examples:

"So I kept on objecting. Finally His Honor says, 'I believe you're in error, counsel, but where's your authority?' I quoted the citation, page and paragraph, even handed him the volume. He read it. His mouth opened in shocked surprise. I swear I heard his uppers fall."

"My client wanted to take the three grand offered. Almost begged me. I sold him on holding out for ten. I had this feeling about that jury. Like a sixth sense. Sure enough, they dumped twelve thou in our lap."

At a social group the gambits run like this:

"That reminds me of a well-known show-biz figure I represented. He didn't know his head from his elbow about contracts. When he saw the deal I worked out for him . . ."

"That reminds me of a client, a political great that was worried shitless about this starlet he knocked up. Neat how I got him off the hook . . ."

"That reminds me of a client charged with paying no income tax—not a penny—on a six figure income. There were a few gimmicks I knew. . . ."

These openers rivet attention. Then outpours the brilliant and heroic gamesmanship that won the day, usually a compound of half-truths and exaggerations.

Pretending to Have What You Lack

> I certainly think it is better to be impetuous than cautious, for fortune is a woman, and it is necessary if you wish to master her, to conquer her by force, and it can be seen that she lets herself be overcome by the bold rather than those who proceed coldly.
>
> —————————————————— *Machiavelli*

It's an ancient gambit, a beautiful tool of deception, used by trial lawyers in civil and criminal cases, and one that you can employ in a wide variety of situations. Counsel will pause in his cross-examination, pick up a document, then address a question to the witness, while looking at a blank paper in his hands. The implication is strong that he already knows the right answer. Few witnesses will hazard a guess or lie under these circumstances; many will accept the answer suggested in the question.

I recently cross-examined a medical witness testifying for the defense in a negligence action:

> *Q.* You have testified many times before in our courts as an expert witness for the defense?
> *A.* I have, on rare occasions.
> *Q.* Would you say five times in the past year?
> *A.* Possibly, but I doubt that many.
> *Q.* How about twelve times?
> *A.* I don't believe that many.
> *Q.* Are you sure, doctor?

The witness hesitated as I picked up a folder and appeared to read it carefully. "I haven't counted them," he replied.

"Wouldn't twenty-one times be more accurate?" I asked, looking at a long sheet that was blank.

He paused. "Possibly."

"In all twenty-one cases, you testified as a witness for the defense, isn't that correct, doctor?"

There was a long pause. "That could be correct."

But this form of deception can backfire. Ephraim Tutt, as defense counsel, offered no objection when the district attorney, in cross-examining the defendant, picked up a copy of *Professional Criminals of America* and holding it so the jury could plainly see the title, opened it and ran his finger down a page, as if reading what he found there.

"Did you not, on September 6, 1927," he demanded, "in company with Red Birch, alias the Roach, Toni Sevelli, otherwise known as Toni the Greaser, and Dynamite Tom Meeghan, crack the safe of the American Railway Express at Rahway, New Jersey, and get away with six thousand dollars?"

The witness denied the charge, but to some of the jurors there must have remained a lingering doubt. Mr. Tutt put the prosecutor on the stand. He addressed a preliminary statement to the bench:

"Your Honor, I have but one question to ask this witness,

and upon his answer I stake my client's liberty. Let him answer any way he sees fit—yes, or no, I care not which—let him make any reply at all which may be officially recorded here and not here—after be disputed or denied by him—and this jury may return a verdict against my client—It is this: Mr. O'Brien, when you took that book in your hand, were you reading something that was printed there or not? YES or NO.'"

Mr. O'Brien, the prosecutor, squirmed and gazed at the floor. If he answered "Yes," insisting he had been reading from the book, and the book was then placed in evidence, he would have been open to a charge of perjury. A "No" answer would obviously destroy the state's case, which it did.[2]

The moral is clear: use caution if you rely on the illusion of possessing what you lack. You could blow your entire game plan.

5. The Research Project

There's no problem so simple a little explanation can't make it complex.
———————————————— *Oscar Levant*

Born in the sciences, research projects have extended into business, education, and government, feeding in the troughs of private and public grants. Many of these are sustained by a variety of put-ons and manipulations that would do credit to Machiavelli.

Two factors make the research stratagem currently attractive:

1. The huge amounts of money made available by philanthropic foundations, government, and industry for research grants; it's like setting out honey pots before a hungry bear.
2. The craze for in-depth studies, and the aura of authenticity that surrounds them.

So if you are an academe or professional with a flair for research, you might consider gathering together a group of similarly qualified individuals for one of the most productive of all put-ons: securing a grant from one of the many well-heeled foundations to conduct a study of a subject within your field. The philanthrophic maneuver is not difficult to put over if you follow a few basic injunctions, suggested in interviews with knowledgeable researchers who have dipped into the trough:

1. Select a foundation that has conducted projects not too dissimilar from the one you have in mind. This you can easily determine by examining the most recent annual report, generally furnished on request, or available in the reference department of large libraries.
2. The project should be described in detail, with sufficient accreditation of its participants to give it a halo of authority.
3. Select a subject not already researched or currently in the hands of a study group. Your librarian can be of considerable help in this area.
4. Remember that your goal is to perpetuate and enlarge, wherever possible; the stated purpose of the project is a secondary and relatively minor factor. Avoid the short-range project, the kind that self-destructs when its first report meets the named problem head-on. Finality is a pronouncement of death to the research plan and those that feed on it.

5. Determine the extent of supervision that will be exercised by those pouring out the money. A project that is too closely monitored, with frequent and detailed progress reports, could expose your own shortcomings and weaken the facade of expertise you have so patiently built. In most cases the research strategist is able to fill his reports with sufficient minutiae, charts, and statistics to impress the unwary with the importance of continuing the labors of his group. Fortunately for you, few of those who administer the grants are knowledgeable enough to distinguish shadow from substance.

6. Cultivate a member of the governing board or committee of the foundation. If he shares some of your enthusiasm for the project, you have gained an unwitting co-conspirator. Decisions about the wisdom of continuing or curtailing the project inevitably arise. Your friend will be reluctant to admit that a mistake was made in the grant, and may as a matter of pride search for reasons to support requests for additional funds. Whether you split any part of the stipend with your friend is your business, but I am sure that also has happened.

7. Learn the Delphic art of communicating without informing. The erudite and voluminous reports submitted should create the illusion that a definitive solution is not far off, and that without a continuance of the project, "all our efforts will be wasted. In a year or two, we hope to offer sufficient data to permit reasonable conclusions to be drawn." You have boxed in the foundation, without committing yourself to a firm cut-off date.

   Your credibility is enhanced at the outset if you point out that "No definitive answers can even be suggested at this time. We must, and will, first determine if the right questions are being asked."

8. Once your project is started, be ever alert for tributaries and offshoots to the main arteries of your research efforts. When found, cast them in a credible mould, like "interesting adjuncts to our principle study, shedding new light on some of the intractable problems." These accessories may mean more jobs, more funds, longer life for the project, even exploration into new and wider fields.

   What if some of the findings in your preliminary reports differ from those currently submitted? Don't be too concerned. The explanation is simple. "Such a variance illustrates the complexity of the problem we are addressing."

9. Write papers for presentation at conventions or meetings in your special field, or for publication in professional journals, reflecting some of the interesting phases of the research project. Few will read them, much less grasp what you have written. Once firmly entrenched, approach the foundation board for funds to subsidize publication of a book or two, "so that the fruits of our labors can inform a wider spectrum of those likely to be affected by the problem under study." The books will give greater credibility to the project and enhance the prestige of the foundation, at least in the eyes of the board members, notwithstanding that its readership will be akin to that for a work on the sex life of amoebic protozoa.

   Arrange for reviews of your books by friendly colleagues, in either professional journals or trade publications. Your stature as an authority will rise, making more unlikely a diminution of funds from the foundations or a query by one of its members: "What has this research team written or done lately?"

I know studies that have been going on for six years, the final report adroitly delayed from year to year for a variety of compelling reasons: "Additional information is needed to adequately formulate a program of action"; "The field under observation has expanded to a depth not previously anticipated"; or the most common reason: "The participants have not yet reached an accord on the recommendations to be made, but are presently reassessing all available data."

A note of caution. Don't intimate that your project may reach conclusions that run counter to well entrenched concepts, unless of course, you are a Nobel Prize winner. You move on thin ice when you disturb sacred cows. A geologist undertook a research project that gave promise of proving there was an abundance of gas and oil in the United States. The Washington hierachy, "captivated by a vision of scarcity," abruptly terminated the project.[1]

It is important to note that research committees are organic rather than mechanical in nature. They are living plants, not structures; rooting, flowering, spreading, scattering their seeds like clusters of weeds, proliferating into offshoots, which in turn grow into more offshoots.

I am aware of one study devoted to rehabilitation of criminals released after serving long prison terms, with particular emphasis upon recidivism. The brainchild of an enterprising law school professor, who enlisted a team of social workers, psychologists, and penologists, the project expanded in three years from six to fourteen participants. The interim reports, wordy and cluttered with imposing statistics, lacked specific conclusions. The paperwork, the office space, and the number of consultants called in from various cities expanded far beyond the original estimates. Team members indulged in recurrent ego trips, with magazine articles, newspaper interviews, and lectures before bar groups, women's clubs, and civic associations.

The head of the project, an impressive figure, reminded me of a tremendous presence in search of a brain. He would be the last to concede that he was grappling with a problem that defies definitive conclusions, one that would bedevil a Solomon and bend a Hercules. The entire project, brilliantly staged, was like a deluxe train looking for a track—which it never found.

Interviews with convicts, prison officials, judges, lawyers, and sociologists ran into the hundreds. Impressive charts and maps lined the office walls. Surely no responsible member of the foundation would entertain the notion of terminating a study steeped so deep in research and enlisting the efforts of so many distinguished experts! I can hear the reply of a team member if such a thought were only vaguely suggested: "After all this effort, all these expenditures, how can one possibly think of terminating the project, and letting the fruits of our labors pour down the drain?"

There was a self-perpetuating beauty to this particular put-on. It graduated a number of its researchers into teaching positions at universities and floated others into other grants with promise of greater longevity. I looked at one of the neatly bound reports of a young lawyer and was dazzled by its weighty comments, the variety of colored graphs and statistics, and the eye-boggling length of the appendix with its citation of authorities and field studies. Surely this chap had answers not given to ordinary man! Actually, he was too deep in the woods to see the trees.

The project finally resulted in a weighty tome, now buried in the reference shelves of law and college libraries. It has not, so far as I can ascertain, added one cubit of knowledge to our understanding of the problems of recidivism and rehabilitation.

So, if you are a professional, a business executive, or someone sufficiently versed in one of the sciences or arts of human endeavors to command respect, gather a few collaborators in your field, equally qualified, and apply to a foundation or government agency for a research grant. They cover a wide range, from studies on the effects on monkeys of prolonged confinement, to the reaction of fish to changes in light and temperature, the progress of twins in the same environment, the effect of weather on bees,[2] consumer reaction to TV commercials; there was even a grant to a group of Southern Illinois educators to measure the effect of blue movies and marijuana on the sexual responses of college sutdents.[3]

Now let us suppose you are a psychologist and have a friend in a government agency concerned with mental health. You want an offbeat research project, one you can do in an offbeat location, like a study of bordellos in Peru.

Farfetched? Hardly. It actually happened. The project was given the Golden Fleece award by Senator Proxmire, the Senate watchdog on wasteful expenditures.[4]

Search your background for *any* expertise on a specific aspect of our modern society. For example, the effects of alcoholism—not on humans (that's been researched down to the bare bone), but let us say, on fish. Wipe away that grin. It was done, by a group that waggled a $102,000 grant to determine whether drunk fish are more aggressive than sober fish. This, too, won a Golden Fleece award in 1976. With good reason. Can you imagine a more pressing problem, with more earth-shattering potential?

No less earth shattering are the results of a study of the sex habits of fiddler crabs, authorized by the Federal government to an Illinois college professor. In applying for the grant, he stated that "although the breeding displays of fiddler crabs have been studied for over 100 years, suprisingly little is known about the development, inheritance and functional significance of these displays."[5] If you don't relate to this profundity, don't feel too bad. Neither do I.

This is not to negate all research projects. A few—pitifully few, in my opinion—match performance to promise. And don't expect prestige and expertise to ensure the marriage. After all, the most heavily researched car in Detroit history was the ill-fated Edsel.

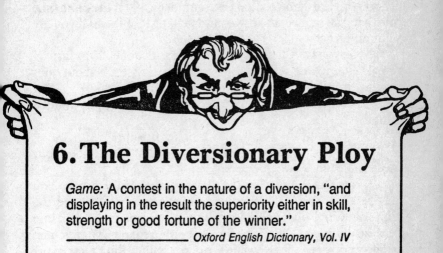

6. The Diversionary Ploy

Game: A contest in the nature of a diversion, "and displaying in the result the superiority either in skill, strength or good fortune of the winner."
———————————— *Oxford English Dictionary, Vol. IV*

I believe it to be most true that it seldom happens that men arise from low condition to high rank without employing either force or fraud. . . .
———————————————— *Machiavelli*

The Mechanics of a Diversion   Deception wears many faces, some barely recognizable. A simple stratagem, easily mastered with a little practice, is the diversionary ploy, used instinctively by lawyers, statesmen and glib-tongued salesmen. With a little practice you can learn how to fuzz an argument while at the same time contriving an irrelevant answer and making it sound as if you are right on target.

"So you have herds of prize cattle and model dairy farms," remarked an American tourist visiting Cuba. "How about your political prisoners?"

"And look at this milking equipment," the guide pointed out.

"Yes, but how about your bulging prisons?"

"Prisons! Prisons!" the guide snapped. "How about your race riots, your sharecroppers?"

Franklin Roosevelt was a master of the sly distraction. You may recall, if you are old enough, how often he skewered the critics of his policies by slipping with magnificent irrelevance into defense of his dog, Fala. The fact that only a single Congressman publicly criticized the Sybaritic life of the animal didn't lessen the effectiveness of FDR's ploy.

See how experienced hands maneuver with this tactic. Governor Pat Brown (Jerry's father) was asked:

"Governor, what's your opinion of the crime rate?"

"Rising crime is not the decisive factor. It's the increasing efficiency of crime reporting, the more accurate computer technology."

A neat dodge, but here's how the son answered the same query:

"Why don't you ask an intelligent question? You sound like you're giving me a Rorschach test—asking me what I think of the crime rate."

A good put-off. I recall President Kennedy being asked at a press conference:

"Mr. President, what is your opinion of the recent Russian proposal for settlement of the nuclear arms controversy?"

"That's a good question, Bill. I can't think of a more pressing problem that cries for solution. It deserves a high priority in our thinking these days."

Incidentally, "That's a good question" is usually followed by a lousy answer. If uncertain of your answer, try replying with your own question.

A pacifist will argue that all wars are immoral, no matter what the purpose. He is asked: "Would you fight in a war if an enemy's soldiers crossed our borders?" The reply: "Who is going to invade our country? Who would dare it with our arsenal of defensive weapons?"

A neat switch and a classic diversion.

Former Governor George Wallace was asked on a talk show: "How about the fiscal deficits in your administration?"

"I'm justly proud of my administration, young man. We built more schools, more roads, more day centers in my four years as Governor than in the past twelve years. It's all in the record."

A neat non sequitur, if you can get away with it. It's endemic before every election. If you're up to your neck in alligators, you can either drain the swamp, or divert attention to something else. The latter is quicker, safer, much easier.

A prospective employer asks a job seeker: "Can you operate the machines you see here?" To answer "No" could blow the job right there.

"I'm very mechanically minded, sir. I repair my own car, fix almost any household appliance, even service most of the TV sets on the market."

You might also try shifting roles.

"Senator, what do you think of this bill?"

"It deserves study, serious study. It's so much like the Hodgson bill introduced before your Committee last month. What did you think of that bill?"

But don't wait for the answer. Plough right on, until you're on safe ground.

A speaker states: "Americans are the best-fed people in the world."

A listener heatedly disputes the statement. "I've seen hunger in the core areas of our cities worse than anywhere else in the world. People picking scraps of food out of garbage cans. Children with bellies bloated from malnutrition. Thousands living on one thin meal a day."

The remarks are totally irrelevant. They are classic diversionary ploys. The speaker did not say that *every* American is well fed. Nor did he deny there are pockets of hunger in our cities. He spoke of the average American, and in that context he was probably correct. But right or wrong, what he said was effectively watered down by the diversion created by his listener.

If you should decide to throw out a red herring, make it strong and compelling. State it emphatically, enough to create the illusion of relevancy. A tepid diversion is too obviously a side-tracking maneuver. If you press down hard enough, you will compel the speaker to meet your argument, thereby creating a side issue. His main point will be lost. If he should return to it, the bruised and mangled carcass may be barely recognizable.

You will not find this basic maneuver of deception in the curriculum of any college or university, or in the self-assertiveness courses that proliferate in increasing numbers each year, or in the books that tell you how to become No. 1 in the corporate hierarchy. Yet the diversionary ploy is not a difficult tactic to master if you will remember a few simple rules:

1. The diversion you select must be at least a distant cousin to the matter you are trying to avoid or water down, not so remote as to be transparently a device to switch attention. In other words, the extraneous issue should bear a credible relationship to the subject under discussion. It can be tenuous, but it must be believable. It can be bizarre in its impact, but it must not appear contrived.

   A classic example is when the sexually frigid wife waters down the passionate urge of her mate, just before and sometimes even during the foreplay.

   "I know, darling, you hate to discuss it, but I'm worried sick about the mounting bills [or the leaking roof, or Junior's poor grades or mother's failing health and where to put her]."

   She has the unerring instinct of a homing pigeon in zeroing in on the right diversion. "Let's talk about it, like two sensible people." His turnoff is quick, irreversible.

   "Why the hell bring that up now?" The resulting argument is enough to cool off a starved Don Giovanni in the heat of passion. He doesn't know exactly what happened, he certainly didn't start it, but everything now is in a flaccid, impotent state. She begins to cry, reducing her anger to self-reproach. The reason for this feeling escapes him.

He knows the maneuver is repetitive, the basic pattern the same, already old hat. But the diversion somehow works, every time.

Occasionally you will hear a diversionary argument that is so perfect that later, when you're thinking over the flaws, you still want to believe it. Your visceral instinct tells you it's hogwash, but you stick loyally to your first impression. That's craftsmanship by the diverter, stupidity by you.

2. Select a diversion that compels attention, holds interest, has some authority. When Clemenceau was asked his opinion of the fourteen points in the charter of the proposed League of Nations, his reply was "Fourteen points! Why the good Lord Almighty only had ten!"

3. Look for a flaw or weakness in the other's remarks, no matter how small. By grabbing it quickly and discussing it at length, you'll divert attention from things you dare not discuss.

Enlarge the minuscule to man-size. Make vigorous objection to a part of the remarks—*any* part. It will probably open an argument, if your objection is not a transparent device to switch attention. The objection may have little or no relevancy to the other's remarks, but if it's handled adroitly, following the suggestions in this chapter, you will have executed a classic diversionary maneuver.

4. In offering the distraction, be unjudgmental of the main issue.

Suppose you are asked: "Should abortions be permitted when pregnancy is the result of rape or incest?" Applying this rule, you avoid a direct answer. There's just too much to be weighed and measured. You're afraid you'll sink in a sea of legal, moral, and philosophical dialectics. How much easier to steer the discussion to the safe harbor of generalities!

"I'm against abortions," you reply. "It's plain murder in most cases, and no right-thinking person condones murder." You haven't answered the question, but you have managed a diversion of sorts.

An indicted associate director of the FBI was asked whether he ever authorized break-ins in pursuit of the fugitive Weathermen in the early 1970's. His reply, as quoted in *The New York Times,* is another classic diversion:

"In my entire career against mobsters and mad bombers, I never approached a case with criminal intent."[1]

He could have added: "I never knowingly broke the law, never committed an illegal act," still without answering the question.

5. Learn how to extend the point of the discussion, thereby steering it from what you'd like to avoid. A simple diversionary ploy, not easily detected. A speaker will argue with you, for example, that some officials in the Labor Department are hostile to unions, using a variety of deceptions to favor management.

"That's not true," you reply. "I can point to a dozen top officials from the Secretary down, who have gone overboard to meet union demands, and to make them more credible." You cite a few cases, neatly diverting attention from the pivotal word "some." Argue long and loud enough and you may bury it in an extended debate.

I have seen witnesses with some courtroom experience use this diversionary maneuver to confuse and exasperate their cross-examiner. This is the evader in action:

"You still haven't answered my question," says counsel.

"Just what is the question?"

Exasperated counsel rephrases the inquiry in more simple language. This time he'll pin him down. The witness is no less determined.

"But that's not the same question you asked me before."

"Please answer it."

"Which one? Your first question or the last one?"

"The last one, please."

"What's the question?"

And so on. If counsel holds on long enough, he'll eventually get the answer he wants, but the effect will be watered down.

6. If your main premise is weak, slip away from it by creating a diversion that supports it and makes it credible, something you can prove without any difficulty. I heard a spirited discussion in California, where I spend part of the year, about a proposed amendment to the state constitution freezing property valuations and promising a rollback of about 60% in property taxes.

"Ridiculous!" a critic argued. "It would wipe out 7 billion—yes, 7 billion—dollars' worth of local government money. Do you know what this will do to libraries, schools, local relief organizations?"

In reply, the proponent dealt at length with the economic suffering of small property owners in recent years, the spiraling sales tax, and other mounting burdens of the Average Citizen. Instead of answering the question: "Should this *specific* proposal pass?" the proponent answered one that might be described as "Is *some* form of taxpayer relief desirable?" It's much easier to support that proposition than the amendment offered and—who knows?—may even become the main subject of discussion.

7. Move from the specific to the general. It gives you more latitude for whatever manipulative tactic you have in mind. For example: "I'm opposed to selling Israel these fighter planes. Must we always bail her out of a tight situation? Must we always correct an imbalance in her weaponry, as measured against her neighbors'?"

This was the argument heard a few years ago from a Midwestern Congressman. He dared not address himself to the specific measure under consideration, the precise need of Israel at that point in time for this shipment of planes. So he escaped into the safety of generalities. A cop-out for politicians and statesmen too lazy or afraid to meet an issue head-on.

These maneuvers are basically one-time ploys. Credibility suffers from repetition. Used too often, this technique casts the user in a mould too easily recognized. Predictability castrates the diversion.

You may well ask at this point: What price credulity?

There are, to be sure, degrees of gullibility, or to put it more politely, susceptibility to your stratagems. What will turn one person on will turn another off. But don't despair. I remember reading somewhere about a single line in *Three Cities* by Sholem Asch, a massive book of over 900 pages, that sticks in my mind: "A single blade of glass is all of Mother Russia." In the same sense, you are basically one of the three billion roaming the face of the earth. You share the same pulses, the same fears, that are buried deep in the genes of all of us.

You Can Learn from Lawyers

. . . from the first he has practiced deception and retaliation, and has become stunted and warped. And so he has

> passed out of youth into manhood; and is now, as he thinks,
> a master in wisdom. Such is a lawyer, Theodorus.
> ——————————————————————————— *Plato*

I attended the law school of a Catholic University, St. Johns in New York City. A course on ethics charted basic moral guidelines; another on trial tactics described basic manipulations in the courtroom. The dichotomy posed some problems for me. I recall a conversation with the teacher of the latter course, an able trial lawyer.

"Suppose you know something," I asked, "that is relevant to the case. Do you make an attempt to disclose it?"

"If it helps your case. Otherwise—no."

"Why not? Isn't a trial a search for justice?"

I recall the white-maned head moving sadly. "No, it's a contest. You're an adversary, and you act the role."

"But isn't it deception to conceal the truth, just to make a point?"

"Not if it will win the case."

I remember pressing further. "Well, what do you do with this thing, this fact that you know could decide the case, or at least have a substantial effect on the outcome?"

"Let it lay. If it surfaces, do all you can to rebut it, or divert attention from it. Diversionary tactic, we call it."

What an intriguing term, and what an arsenal of deceptions it conceals! Let me describe some of them, as practiced by trial lawyers. With a little imagination, you can adapt them to a wide range of manipulations in your everyday activities.

You can acquire more insight into the diversionary tactic from trial lawyers than any other craft, including politicians and statesmen, who rank as amateurs by comparison. This is part of the closing argument of Clarence Darrow in the Bill Heywood trial:

> Who is it that pleads for justice for Bill Heywood? Who waits for hours in the cold and rain for the courthouse to open? It's the poor and weary workers, downtrodden and old before their time. I ask you to look at their faces, these forgotten people. They look to you now for simple justice in this case.

The gut issue of guilt or innocence was never met head-on. In its place, Darrow raised the spectre of the poor being bled by the rich, the downtrodden under the heel of the powerful.

It is difficult to see any relevancy between the servitude of the working class and the guilt or innocence of Bill Heywood. But the diversionary tactic worked—as do many similar appeals today for defendants from minority groups. Darrow, in effect, created a collateral issue: justice to the poor and downtrodden. And as any lawyer on the weaker side of a case knows, the more diversionary issues he raises, the better his chances for a verdict. Ephraim Tutt aptly remarked in *Yankee Lawyer:* "There's no proposition of law too foolish or absurd to advance to a judge and no claim as to fact too foolish for a jury to swallow."[2]

Take for example, a time-worn defense in rape cases, a diversion to water down culpability. Counsel will try hard to get something, *anything*, on the complainant, that will lessen her credibility. Prior indiscretions are ripe plums, on the theory that a woman who has been penetrated before will suffer less. Even if counsel does not have hard facts to support his supposition, he is often not above imputing it. Jurors won't admit it, but raping a prostitute is not the same as raping a schoolteacher.

Counsel's low point is usually at the high point of his opponent's summation or closing argument to the jury. He must sit quietly and listen as the weaknesses of his case are stripped clean, and his mistakes exaggerated out of all proportion.

But not all sit quietly. A few try to break the spell by ruffling through their files, fumbling anxiously for something that is never found (the "lost paper" technique), persistent coughing despite gulps of water, reading memos slipped to the counsel table and scribbling replies, or just staring loud and hard at several jurors, alternately smiling and frowning, scratching the head, and wriggling the brows in pained disbelief at remarks made by counsel.

A master at diversion was Clarence Darrow, who would tilt his chair back and snap his galluses at the height of his opponent's summation. A favorite tactic was to bend over and hold his head in a gesture of incredulity that anyone could mouth such untruths.

He played the "ham" to perfection. At the end of a criminal trial, as the district attorney began his summation, Darrow moved his chair near the jury and lit up a cigar. In those days smoking was permitted in some courts. He held it high for the jury to see, never flicking the ashes as he puffed away. The gray end grew longer and longer, holding the fascinated gaze of the jury, and diverting their attention. A thin wire inserted the length of the cigar held the ashes intact. At the climax of the prosecutor's summation, Darrow stopped puffing and just stared at the long ash, as if to share the jury's mounting curiosity.[3]

A common diversionary stratagem of trial counsel is to find a weakness no matter how minute, in his opponent's case, then shine it, polish it, blow it up out of all proportion to its importance, and hope it diverts attention from the losers in his case. Or, no less effective, unearth *something, anything,* that will obscure what he wants obscured, and that he can somehow get over to the jury, even if it's totally irrelevant to the gut issues.

> A remarkable man indeed, the trial lawyer; the embodiment of honor and truth, edged with deception and framed in cunning phrase.
>
> ——————————————— *Samuel Johnson*

If you ever sit on a jury or attend a trial, you'll observe how counsel, if he's an experienced hand, will almost invariably follow at least one of two simple stratagems in his closing remarks:

1. He will introduce diversionary or side issues in an attempt to divert attention from strong points made by the opposition, for which you sense he had no adequate reply, or
2. He will select the weakest part of his opponent's argument and exaggerate it out of all proportion to its importance, while ignoring issues that cry for discussion.

The diversionary gambits of yesteryear are likely to appear transparent today. The widespread exposure of the public to the contrived TV courtroom dramas, and the spawn of books on famous courtroom exploits by the greats at the criminal bar, have served to make juries too familiar with the tactics of lawyers during a trial. For example, picture this tableau of a bygone era:

A defendant charged with a fiendish murder. His counsel,

aware of the modest circumstances of juries serving in that area, sitting in his hotel room the night before the trial, rubbing the elbows of his jacket with sandpaper until they are threadbare, scuffing his shoes, and planning the most minute details for an unkempt appearance at the trial.

Yet that was Clarence Darrow's classic diversion in his defense of a man accused of a muder—a crime with no redeeming feature. As described by one observer, his appearance the following morning was simply too much for the prosecutor. Darrow played his role with Shakespearian skill, hanging his head slightly, sneaking an eye-corner view of the jurors, surmising that they, brothers under their unkempt attire, were genuinely sorry for him. It was all over but the verdict. An acquittal followed.

The era of Bill Fallon and Earl Rogers saw many innovative manipulations of witnesses, aimed at creating diversions. The diversionary ploys are no less popular today among the trial bar, but they are infinitely more sophisticated.

Can you, for example, envision Edward Bennet Williams arranging for his client, at a prearranged signal, to break into sobs during his direct examination—as did Fallon in his heyday—and then, pulling out a handkerchief to stem the flow of tears, allow a rosary to fall to the floor in front of the jury? Several of the jurors were obviously touched to the point of tears. An acquittal followed.[4]

Not so subtle, but equally effective, was the diversionary tactic of Earl Rogers in his defense of an alleged hotel thief, accused of stealing a ring valued at only a few dollars but prized for sentimental reasons. The defendant appeared in court, a quiet and well-dressed man, wearing a large ring set with fine diamonds, and an expensive looking cravat bearing a pin of white stone flanked by several blood red rubies. A heavy gold chain was draped across his embroidered vest, fastened to a gold watch that he occasionally consulted.[5]

No allusion was made by counsel to the defendant's costly jewelry and expensive attire, except for an occasional remark about the rashness of accusers generally, causing needless shame and expense to innocent people. The jurors could not suppress their amused smiles at the absurdity of the whole proceeding, that a well-to-do gentleman would stoop to stealing a three-dollar ring. He was quickly acquitted.

Even less subtle was the ingenious distraction used by the wily Earl Rogers in a murder trial where the prosecutor's closing remarks were effectively destroying a defense which, at best, could be described as contrived. As was his custom, Rogers left his assistant in the courtroom while he strolled the corridor outside, occasionally pausing at the door to hear the State's summation. Growing increasingly disturbed at what he heard, Rogers suddenly burst into the courtroom and rushed to his youthful assistant, abusing him in strident tones. The courtroom was thrown into confusion. The prosecutor stopped in the middle of his peroration. An astonished judge rapped for order.

As if suddenly aware of his disruptive conduct, Rogers now became a picture of abject contrition. He apologized profusely to the judge, the jury and the prosecutor, explaining that his associate had failed to follow instructions and object to improper remarks in the summation of the state's attorney. When he finished his apologies, done with gracious bows, the prosecutor tried to resume his summation, but finally raised his hands in a gesture of surrender.

"I have been a prosecutor for thirty-five years, but this is the first time I have ever engaged in a trial where defense counsel made the final argument to the jury."[6]

The jurors forgot the climax he had tried too hard to reach and returned with a verdict of acquittal.

A favorite diversionary tactic of Howe and Hummel, famed New York criminal lawyers at the turn of the century, was to engage a buxom woman to sit in the front row of the courtroom, eyes glued to the defendant, and always moving close to him during the recess. She was invariably sad-faced, and poorly dressed, and often held a baby in her arms. Tears flowed freely during the final argument, with an occasional wail from the infant. We can only conjecture how many jurors succumbed to this masquerade.

I represented a motorist injured in a highway accident. The defendant driver, an elderly woman, had been carefully coached by her lawyer, a shrewd counsel who represented a string of insurance companies. I began my cross-examination:

> Q. Do I understand you correctly, from the time you left your house until this accident you did not drive over fifteen miles an hour?

A. That is correct; most of the time it was only ten miles an hour.

Suspecting a possible car defect or a physical impairment, I ventured further, which was a disastrous mistake.

Q. You knew the speed limit was fifty-five miles an hour?

A. Yes, but the rear of my car had fifty jars of preserves that I canned for St. Anthony's Christmas Dinner for the Needy, and I didn't want to see them broken.

A good Samaritan who goes to the trouble of cooking and canning fifty jars of preserves for the hungry poor is certainly not capable of negligent driving. Any juror knows that.

A beautiful diversion—carefully rehearsed by opposing counsel—credible enough to sink my case.

Less obvious, but infinitely more effective, are the diversionary ploys counsel creates in his closing remarks to the jury. Some trial counsel have an uncanny ability to divert the attention of the jury from weaknesses in their case, by beclouding and confusing the central issue, often using what passes for Aristotelian logic.

A wide range of diversionary tactics are employed. Louis Nizer was confronted with this challenge in the famous libel suit of Quentin Reynolds against Westbrook Pegler. He described to the jury the myriad of diversions offered by the defense, which apparently recognized its inability to meet head-on the plaintiff's contentions.

"How does defense counsel handle this kind of situation? He does precisely what my opponent has so skillfully done. He attempts from the very outset of the trial to becloud the issue, to avoid any discussion of the facts, never to discuss the truth, but to bring in every conceivable kind of prejudicial issue.

"It is something like the octopus. When it is attacked and is fearful of its life, it ejects a black inky fluid. The water all around becomes black, enabling the octopus to escape its enemy.

"That is what, from the opening of the trial to this very point, defense counsel has so skillfully done; he has emitted black fluid to confuse you and hide the real issues in this case."

The jury agreed with Nizer and awarded Reynolds a substantial verdict.

By this time, the trial lawyer's diversionary tactics should have taught you a few rules for practicing the Machiavellian art of deception:

Never respond from weakness to a position with which you disagree—for the same reasons an experienced trial lawyer will never place himself in a weak or defensive posture in answering a challenge posed by his adversary. If you have no credible answer, follow one of two courses:

1. Make no direct reply; don't try using a water pistol to put out a raging fire.
2. Create a diversionary issue. This tactic is in the best tradition of debate, argument, trial advocacy, or any forensic art.

Should you be inclined to question the applicability of these maneuvers to your business, political, or professional activities, don't. I have used them in areas as distant as the moon from legal gamesmanship—and they work. Not always, of course, but more often than you might imagine.

Promises, Promises

> His promises were, as he then was, mighty; But his performance, as he is now, nothing.
>
> —————————————— *Shakespeare: Henry VIII*

A beneficent promise can divert attention from something you want another to overlook, as for example your inability to perform in a specific situation. The well-intentioned commitment is beyond our discussion—in fact, it needs none. But what of the promise born of expediency? The desire to manipulate?

To succeed in such a venture, three simple caveats must be observed:

1. Fulfillment must be far enough in the future to enable you to reap the benefits of your promise; a premature demand for you to redeem could ruin your game plan.
2. The promise must not be impossible or incredible on its face; it must be grounded in plausibility.
3. If your promises are multiple, don't mingle the believable

       with the unbelievable. A chain of commitments is no
       stronger in believability than its weakest link.
4. Balance future consequences of your default against
       present benefits. Don't mortgage the future for a low
       current return. You may execute a brilliant diversionary
       maneuver, but invite a Draconian denouement when you
       can't make good your promise.

Draw a lesson from a master in this manipulation. Jimmy Carter
affords a classic example of promises adroitly used as a diversionary ploy and a good put-on. His strategy, brilliantly conceived
and executed, succeeded in its basic aim: to divert attention from
the controversial issues and his own inability to deal adequately
with them. He promised in his campaign to support efforts for a
Palestinian homeland in the Middle East, "a legitimate aspiration
of a long-suffering people"; he assured Israel we would bend
every effort to preserve its "territorial integrity" and help it resist
invaders; he made firm promises to reduce government agencies
and the White House staff (they have actually increased); he
made promises to attract votes of the Southern Yahoos, the liberal
Northeasterners, the integrationists, the segregationists, the
Midwest farmers, and the Wall Street moneybags.

    True, his promises elected him. He apparently complied
with all four of the above injunctions. There was no date set for
fulfillment—that was a comfortable distance ahead; the promises were all eminently plausible, none patently unbelievable. But
there is a growing fear that he may overlook the last caveat.

    Jimmy succeeded admirably in diverting attention from
his own inadequacy in meeting these problems. In fact, quite the
reverse: his maneuvers pointed to statesmanlike qualities and an
innate honesty. "If ever I lie to you, if ever I mislead you, then
don't vote for me, because I won't be worthy of your vote if I'm
not worthy of your trust."

    But even the most charitable view of our President today
raises serious questions as to his ability. The time for payment on
his promises has long since passed. La Rochefoucauld put it
neatly when he said: "We promise according to our hopes and
perform according to our fears."

    Unfortunately, that describes the present dilemma of
President Carter. You can learn from his predicament.

7. One-Upmanship, Forget It

Whoever exalts himself shall be humbled.
Matthew 23:12

In old days nobody pretended to be a bit better than his neighbors. In fact, to be a bit better than one's neighbors was considered excessively vulgar and middle-class. Nowadays, with our modern mania for morality, everyone has to pose as purity, incorruptibility . . . and what is the result?
Oscar Wilde: An Ideal Husband

Winners Always Lose

> The writer I dislike the most is Shakespeare, when I compare my mind to his.
> ———————————————— *George Bernard Shaw*

Since the manipulations you have in mind may not be entirely honorable by conventional standards, you sorely need credibility and trust at the outset. And a sure way to get neither is to create a dominant role by demonstrating that the other's statements are wrong, stupid, or plain crazy, and that you're the superior.

If you're one up, he's one down, and that's no way to start a relationship. No one likes a smartass. The art of cleverness is to know how to conceal it. If you have a unique talent for puns, cutting jibes, or quickies about sexual acrobatics, forget it. They are only preludes to one-upmanship (especially if the other is an envious clod), and that won't help your quest one bit.

> 'Tis a great ability to know how to conceal one's ability.
> ———————————————— *La Rochefoucauld*

Almost all relationships establish, with varying degrees of subtlety, a dominant role. This does not imply "superior" in social status or economic position, or even intellectual prowess. The most menial servant can sometimes maneuver neat put-downs of his master.

No precise definition exists for the ingredients of one-upmanship; the term is relative and is being continually defined and redefined with each new relationship. But there is an instinctive awareness of when you are one-up, and you can trust this instinct in guiding you to avoid verbal or nonverbal moves casting you in this role. They make your quest much more difficult.

Still, there are situations where your "superiority" or dominance will emerge, clear if not loud, no matter how hard you try to conceal it—particularly in your nonverbal communications. The trick here is not to struggle to avoid the unavoidable, or conceal what cannot be concealed, but to clothe it in the least objectionable form, never forgetting that a transparent humility won't radiate sincerity. It won't radiate honesty. It just won't radiate.

"I'm not disagreeing with you, but . . ."

"In my humble opinion . . ."

"I don't have all the answers, but on this point . . ."

"Far be it for me to say, but . . ."

"I don't think you're listening to what I'm saying."

"It's really simple, if you'll just listen to me."

These transparencies, or their variants, are signals to your listener. Stretch them too far, and you resemble an imposing figure standing on a raised platform, frame stretched to its fullest, chest puffed, and proclaiming in a stentorian voice: "I'm not a man given to boasting, but in my humble opinion . . ."

The Quaker creed: No pomp under any circumstance.

A physicist was recently asked to testify on the long-range effects of nuclear waste buried deep underground. His attitude was condescending, slightly irritating. He began: "In my humble opinion," at which point a questioner from the audience interrupted: "No one is interested in a 'humble,' 'proud,' or any other kind of opinion. Just tell us in plain words, can this damned stuff be safely buried underground, and how."

To paraphrase Mark Twain: "Affectation of any kind is a language that the deaf can hear and the blind can read."

Whether it's a bumpkin or know-it-all you're trying to persuade, you're putting up roadblocks when you contradict or demean what he is saying, verbally or nonverbally, even if you know it's infantile or pure bullshit. Instead of a head-on crash, try an end run:

"There's a lot to what you say . . ."

"You've got some good points there . . ."

Where you can't restrain yourself and simply must reply, begin by including yourself:

"That's something I never knew."

"You're right there. That's a problem we all neglected."

"I could be wrong. I often am."

"Let's look at it this way."

Leave just enough room to slip gracefully with what you're going to say. Shade your doubts to a bare hint you're not in 100%

agreement. If you want to make a man your enemy, just tell him "You're wrong, dead wrong." It works every time.

Not only the Orientals value "face." Face is important to everyone, no matter how illusory the saving factor. A labor conciliator put it this way: "I always give my decision to one side and the language to the other."

The maneuvering to get on top can range from crude to subtle, one no less ego-wrecking than the other. And it isn't confined to pegging your intellectual capacity, wealth, or social status. It's also in the way you shade a question or remark. For example:

"Do you see what I mean?"

"Have I made myself clear?"

"Maybe if I put it this way, you'll see what I'm getting at."

"Yes, but . . ."

You're implying a degree of obtuseness, subtle but jagged, and that, my friend, is polluting the soil in which you hope to plant the seed of your deception. Trial lawyers dread a show of brilliance as much as stupidity. Tenacity and honesty, yes, but never the Olympian superiority, the pedantic, patronizing intelligence. It's infinitely better if you can create the illusion you are the victim of one-upmanship. As one advertising man put it: "The biggest help in selling is to give the public the illusion it's screwing you."

Real rape is forcible entry. Verbal rape is a veiled process of deception. Try to force your way in with subtle ridicule or argument, and all you'll work up is a good sweat.

To verbally seduce, it's senseless to play one-upmanship with the intended victim of your bluff or deception. You beguile him, you entice him, you praise and induce him, but you never belittle him.

Exclusivity is just as objectionable. So you belong to a restricted club or group that your listener does not. Unless the subject of your conversation requires that you disclose it—*don't*. It pegs you a notch higher than your listener. Carl Sandburg was asked for a list of bad words. He replied that he knew of only one: "*Exclusive*." It makes the speaker feel superior, he explained, and the other a little inferior.

And that's no way to establish a good rapport.

> It is advisable at times to feign folly, as Brutus did, and this
> is sufficiently done by praising, speaking and doing things
> contrary to your way of thinking.
>
> ————————————————————————— *Machiavelli*

Where your listener is obviously out in left field, arguing about
something totally unrelated to what you are saying, draw him out,
try to swing him to the core issue. Hopefully, he will see that you
and he are not in the same ball park. And if his opposition grows
vehement, let it run its course. Don't jump too fast to match his
intensity or show up his stupidity. Because in this game, winners
always lose.

No less objectionable is The Moralistic Pose:

"I'd never do it that way. It's against my sense of justice."

"I think I know the moral from the immoral. And this is
immoral, believe me."

"You don't have to be a reborn Christian—which incidentally I am—to know this is wrong."

"Deception is something I've never practiced. I wasn't
raised that way."

"So he made a bundle on the deal. I don't envy him. 'What
is a man profited, if he shall gain the whole world and lose his own
soul?'"

You're elevating yourself, subtly but surely, above the
common herd. And that is classic up-manship. You haven't en-
deared yourself one cubit. Nobody likes the sight of a halo on
another. Never forget that we're all opportunists at heart,
camouflaging it behind a myriad of pretenses and holier-than-
thou expressions.

> Nature hath put this tincture
> in our blood,
> That each would be a tyrant
> if he could.
>
> ————————————————————————— *Daniel Defoe*

Be particularly careful to avoid the most common impediment to
any manipulative maneuver—falling into the trap of ego-speak.
Listen carefully to some of the conversation around you. Note
how much of the content is ego-speak (an apt term from a book by

that name). Out of a ten-minute talking span, five may be devoted to massaging the ego of the speaker, at the expense of any meaningful persuasion. He assumes he is describing things or people, when actually he is talking about his own unique talents or deeds, and proving himself a first class pain in the *a* double *s*. The persuasive effect is about the same as reading the Gettysburg Address.

Never Win An Argument To implant a new thought in another, to create a desire or shape an attitude, is the *sine qua non* of deception. But you won't do it by winning an argument.

Crafty Ben Franklin, a master at verbal seduction, put it neatly in his autobiography:

> I made it a rule to forebear all direct contradiction to the sentiments of others, and all positive assertion of my own. I even forbid myself. . . the use of every word or expression in the language that imported a fix'd opinion, such as certainly, undoubtedly, etc., and I adopted, instead of them, I conceive, I apprehend, or I imagine a thing to be so or so; or it so appears to me at present.

When you argue, you put one opinion against another. Yours against his. Opinions fit comfortably, like an old hat or pair of shoes. If what you say is so logical, so irrefutable, it knocks hell out of the other's stand, it means he must realign his thinking, dropping old ideas for new.

This is not always done easily or quickly. Pride dies hard. Suppose the other's reply misses the point of discussion by a mile, still it's a reply. *His* reply. And when you oppose it or subtly ridicule it, you could be lighting the small flame of an argument. Even if the other nods his head in polite agreement, the flame remains, growing with each thrust you make.

So you win the argument. You've silenced the other. What exactly have you won? You've exposed an error or fallacy in the other's thinking, compelled him to change an opinion or attitude he may have nurtured for a long time. That's never pleasant. He may respect you more, but he'll like you less. True, you're one up, but strategically you're one down.

What did you lose? The rapport necessary to put over whatever manipulative maneuver you had in mind.

I recall a discussion at a cocktail party not too long ago.

"History is full of Watergates," someone remarked. "Wasn't it Lord Acton who said: 'All power tends to corrupt'?"

A mousy little man added: "And absolute power corrupts absolutely."

"I never heard that," the first speaker said.

"Few people have."

A discussion ensued, overheard by the host, who lifted *Bartlett's Familiar Quotations* from a bookshelf. There it was. That's what the man said.

Mr. Smarty made his point—at a price.

Not unlike the quotation I once offered in a conversation: "Isaiah put it well—'Many that are first shall be last.'"

"You're wrong," Mr. God interrupted, "on both counts. The quote is 'And the last shall be first,' Book of Matthew."

So my friend knew the Bible better than I did. What did he accomplish? He climbed a foot higher in his reputation for biblical knowledge—but he became infinitely less likeable.

Small potatoes, you'll say, a trivial incident. True, but it did make a dent in the other's ego. And even the tiniest crack will make your quest that much more difficult.

So, whether you're trying to make a sale or win a point at the dinner table, don't try to be one-up by showing the other wrong. There are more effective gambits, as this chapter points out.

Politicans and debaters obviously play a different game. To them, arguments are weapons, not to persuade or establish the truth of a proposition, but to show their supremacy.

Lose your cool in an argument and you'll make the best rebuttal you'll ever regret. Even if, with your bombast, sharp wit, or sheer logic, you clobber the other into a submissive acknowledgment that you're right, you've diminshed his ego. You see this every day in arguments raised to the point where the paramount concern is to beat down or humiliate the other.

Argument generates heat but no warmth, even if you're contesting with an idiot. To argue with a fool is to become one.

Forget the high school debates you took such delight in, the traps you laid for your opponent, the Aristotelian maneuvers for discrediting his major premise. These were affairs staged for specific purpose: the winning of an argument. You won if you convinced the judges you had the better of it, but the game rules in the school auditorium bear as much resemblance to real life as bush-league tryouts to a World Series.

Yes, there are exceptions. If you are a corporate executive, for example, anxious to score in the eyes of the Big One at a conference or board meeting, you will wield your sword at every opportunity, in varying degrees of subtlety, of course. Whatever puts you one-up for recognition or promotion, and your rivals one-down, is not only permissible, but good strategy. The road to advancement in the organizational jungle is littered with the corpses of the knowledgable but inarticulate.

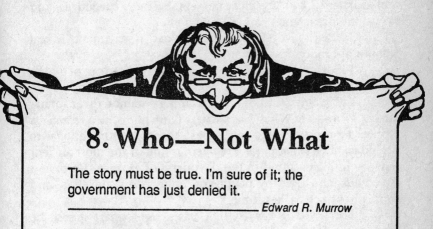

8. Who—Not What

The story must be true. I'm sure of it; the government has just denied it.
———————————————————— *Edward R. Murrow*

On the decline of the Great Tao,
The doctrines of "humanity" and "justice" arose.
When knowledge and cleverness appeared,
Great hypocrisy appeared in its wake.[1]
———————————————————— *The Wisdom of Laotse*

So you're unable to readily disprove or challenge what another is saying? Don't despair, and don't try matching his hand with the clinkers you hold. There's a simple maneuver, instinctive for some, foreign to many, but learnable by all. Try discrediting the one saying it, or the authority he quotes to support his view. It's a tool sharpened by statesmen, lawyers, business executives, and brimstone preachers.

"I like the way Jones runs that new department. A real smooth operation."

"Fiddlesticks. I know for a fact he was booted out of his last job for inefficiency."

A gold nugget of deception, and a common diversionary tactic. "Who—Not What" has a stately Latin title of *ad verecundiam* (appeal to prestige). It's fairly close to *ad hominem*, appeal to prejudice. The *ad hominem* stratagem is one of the most ancient fallacies in logic, found in the discourses of Horace, Plato, and Aeschylus, and used by politicians, editorialists, novelists, and dramatists since earliest time.

"For a young lawyer, that was a right smart speech he made to the jury."

"It wasn't so hot. How could it be? He not only graduated from a third-rate law school, I heard he finished near the bottom of his class."

This deceptive maneuver is easy to identify, and easy to use because we tend to think more about the personality a speaker projects than the argument he presents.

"I like what he proposed. It made sense."

"Hogwash. It was plain stupid. The man never went beyond the fifth grade."

You could barely fill a thimble with the logic in most of the oratory in political campaigns. But we instinctively buy the man for the illusion of competency he projects; what he says can be more nonsense than sense. Anybody as homespun and freshly minted as Jimmy Carter simply had to be The Man for the Job. It wasn't what was said, so much as *who* said it.

It's an ironic truth that given a choice, we select the comfortable familiarity of the illogical or irrational; the logical is accepted only when no alternative is offered.

You may recall the prologue to *Fanny's First Play* by Bernard Shaw. A drama critic is asked to comment on the production, the name of the playwright being omitted. "How can I tell if it's a good play," he replies, "if I don't even know who wrote it?"[2]

And when Joe Namath recommends a sports shirt, or Miss America a beauty aid, they are using *ad hominem* proof. The reasons for buying are largely ignored. You are being deceived by appeals totally unrelated to the merits of the product.

The logical fallacy of *ad hominem,* properly used, diverts attention from the gut issue *(ad rem)* by attacking directly or by innuendo, the speaker's character, ability or accomplishments.

"Who—Not What" Paste this credo in your hat the next time you prepare to enter a lively discussion. But the Squid Squirt, as I call this tactic, can't be used indiscriminately. Here are a few suggestions:

1. It must not be framed in obvious malice, lest your strategy become immediately evident. When Roosevelt's critics attacked a government proposal because it came from "that cripple in the White House," *ad hominem* became *ad disaster.*

    And when a reporter interviewed a Midwest Congressman sympathic to the Arab cause, he asked him about one of Begin's peace proposals.

    "It's unfair and totally unrealistic."

    "In what respects, Congressman?" he was asked.

    "Do you need a bill of particulars?" he retorted, with some heat. "Just look at the man's record, his background. He was a terrorist, a mad bomber. What can you expect from that kind of a leader? Only violence and more violence."

    "But his proposal—"

    "It's no damn good. How could it be?"

    A neat turn-off, but framed in such hostility and malice, the gnat-size brain of the Congressman lost whatever credibility it might otherwise have. A wasted who-not-what maneuver.

2. Don't be too quick to use the maneuver. The proposition you are trying to discredit may be so tenuous it will topple of its own weight. Or it may be so flimsily constructed it falls apart under a frontal attack using *ad rem.* In either of these events, discrediting the speaker or the authority he relies upon could be needless mayhem.

3. Don't belabor the point; make it and leave it. I was told of

an incident where the division manager in a large tool plant resisted the Board's proposal to hire a management consultant.

"Not him, good Lord! He's strictly bush league. I'm familiar with his training and experience." That was more than enough to sink the proposal. But the speaker was not satisfied. "Let me tell you about some of his jobs." He bore down so hard his motive became immediately suspect. The Board listened politely, reserved decision, eventually hired the consultant.

4. Be sure of your facts. Don't speculate, exaggerate, or fabricate. The imposing facade built by that master of *ad hominem,* the late Senator Joseph McCarthy, eventually collapsed under its burden of lies and distortions. In more temperate hands, his who-not-what tactic, with its sly innuendoes, might have succeeded in its objectives. Unfortunately it buried too many innocent victims.

   If the accuracy of your diversion is skewered by whomever it's directed against, you're in the same discredited position as McCarthy. Whatever you say after that will have the same effect as quoting the Old Testament to a Communist dialectician.

5. Where there is the slightest chance that your attack will generate sympathy, forget it. The risk far outweighs any possible benefits. I have seen brilliant cross-examinations in court thoroughly vitiated by the sympathy they aroused for the witness.

6. Your remarks must bear some relationship, however tenuous, to the matter under discussion. You won't discredit your competitor for an executive job by citing his lousy golf score or his parking tickets, although Abe Lincoln used a bit of far-out trivia to good advantage in one of his first jury trials. His oratorical opponent, an experienced trial lawyer, had the stronger case. It was a warm day, with Lincoln slumped deep in his chair, looking for a winning gambit. It came when his opponent took off his coat, showing one of the city slicker shirts of that period, which buttonted up the back.

   The wily Abe saw the puzzlement on the face of the jury, made up of frontiersmen. His final plea was brief, but enough to turn the case in his favor: "Gentlemen of the jury, since I have justice on my side, I know you will not be influenced by this gentleman's pretended legal

knowledge. Why, you can see he doesn't even know which
side of his shirt ought to be in front!"[3]

You may recall the furor over the nomination of David
Lilienthal in 1947 as the first Chairman of the Atomic
Energy Commission. His writings and speeches were
brilliant, admired worldwide for their erudition. But the
senior senator from Tennessee, a 100% American patriot,
bitterly attacked Lilienthal's qualifications, labeling him a
dangerous man, not to be trusted in this highly sensitive
post, because his parents were born in Hungary, a nation
now under Communist control.

A powerful word, *patriot*. With barely any practice, you
can learn how to hide behind it in bedeviling someone or
something you don't like.

Any true American knows, for example, the insidious
influence of a painting done by a Communist sympathizer.
Consider the series of paintings by celebrated artists
collected by *Sports Illustrated* and scheduled for exhibition
in 1956 at the Museum of Fine Arts in Dallas. Alerted to
the threat to American freedoms, the Dallas County
Patriotic Council strongly opposed the exhibition,
pointing out that four of the artists were once members of
a Communist front organization, and that Communist art
is traditionally used to brainwash public attitudes. The
paintings of the four artists showed: a winter scene, a
baseball game, an elderly fisherman, and a group of ice
skaters.

The trustees of the museum finally decided to conduct
the exhibition. The patriots of Dallas County braced
themselves for a tide of Communist sympathizers, which it
is reliably reported has so far not materialized.

An extreme case? Hardly. You'll remember, if you're
old enough, how *The Thin Man*, a superb detective story,
was removed from some library shelves because the author
took the Fifth Amendment before a Congressional
committee. The book had as much political implication as a
McGuffey reader.

The who-not-what deception begins early in life. I
recall a jigsaw puzzle completed by one of my grandsons.
"Looks perfect," I commented. The other grandson,
without looking at the layout, said:

"It's all wrong."

"Where is it wrong?" I asked.

"All over. He never does things right."

7. If you are the target in a who-not-what maneuver, be prompt in your counterattack.

I spoke several years ago at a town meeting, in opposition to a proposed change in a zoning ordinance, allowing light business in a residential area. A proponent took issue with my remarks. The debate grew heated.

"You opposed funds for expansion of the high school," he angrily remarked. "It passed. You opposed hiring an assistant town engineer. He was hired. Doesn't that tell us something?"

"It sure does," I replied. "You win some, lose some. Now you tell me, what the hell does that have to do with the question now before us?"

There are three classes of intellects: one which comprehends by itself, another which appreciates what others comprehend, and a third which neither comprehends by itself or by the showing of others; the first is excellent, the second good, the third, useless.

—————————————————————— *Machiavelli*

Then there is the nagging question of ethics or fair play. When is it morally wrong to attack what a speaker is, in order to discredit what he says? A neat question, not easily answered. Let us suppose you are constrained by moral considerations and want to play the game fair and square.

If you know the speaker is parroting the views of a special group, or his background and associations make questionable what he is saying, or his present views differ from those previously expressed, use *ad hominem*. But if you lack such pay dirt, and all you can dig up to justify your mayhem is a dislike of the person, his dress, his personality, or the fact that he's rich and good looking and you're not, stick to what he is saying, not what he is.

Then there are situations where not only is reliance on the ad hominem maneuver ethically correct, but it would be wrong not to use it. You learn, for example, that your opponent for the job of town treasurer was discharged years ago as a supermarket cashier for robbing the till. Should you disclose it, or let the past lie buried?

Distinctions can become blurred, if you're a stickler for principle. Grover Cleveland's illegitimate son was used against him in the Presidential campaign. A classic who-not-what attack. The voters rejected the argument, deciding that the candidate's virtues overshadowed his single indiscretion. The tactic was as logical as using former Congressman Hay's sexual peccadillos to attack his stand on foreign policy.

Who-not-what is a favorite, if not indispensable, ingredient of legal gamesmanship. The law traditionally supports, if not legitimatizes, the maneuver. "What you have been, and what you have done in the past, speaks as loud as what you are now testifying if not louder." True, and not true.

Your story on the witness stand could be accurate in all respects, and yet be robbed of credibility by your prior misdeeds. Conversely, a fabrication from the lips of a clergyman or a revered public figure can sound like the Word of God. The fact that you were convicted of wife beating should not logically stamp what you now say as unbelievable, but it may, and often does. You're less likeable, less worthy of belief. And the disclosure that you were previously convicted of perjury in an entirely different case does not prove you are lying now—but try telling that to a jury. Your credibility as a witness is forever undermined.

"Tell me, Mr. Jones, were you ever convicted of a crime?"

"Yes, many years ago."

"What was that crime?"

Counsel already has the details, but this is too choice a morsel to be swallowed in one gulp.

"Perjury."

"That means, of course, that you lied under oath?"

The witness paused. How much blood does the bastard want?

"Yes, I suppose so."

"And you now want this jury to believe that the testimony you gave this morning is the truth?"

And so on, stripping the witness of believability, until it would take a miracle of faith for the jury to accept anything he said, even if documented by the College of Cardinals.

A medical witness with impressive credentials confronted a cross-examiner who groped futilely for an opening. About to dismiss the witness, he turned and abruptly asked:

124 WHO—NOT WHAT

Q. What is your full name, doctor?
A. A. Taylor White.
Q. Your *full* name, please.
A. You just heard it.
Q. What does the "A" stand for?
A. I never use it.
Q. I know that, but please, doctor, answer my question.
   After an embarrassing pause, the answer came:
A. Abraham.
Q. Why are you ashamed of "Abraham," doctor?

To Jews on the jury, the witness shrank in size.

The sturdy appearance of the defendant, accused of a robbery, belied his physical condition. He was suffering from a cancer of the throat. His voice, slightly coarse, was purposely kept low, barely audible. For me to disclose the condition was improper—it was obviously not relevant to his guilt or innocence.

Yet there was no difficulty in communicating the condition to the jury, even baiting the prosecutor to invite the disclosure during his cross-examination of the defendant.

Q. Can you hear my questions?
A. Yes, I can.
Q. Then will you please speak a little louder, so the jury can hear you.
A. I'll try, but you see, I have throat cancer, and it makes it hard for me to talk loud.

The court promptly granted the prosecutor's motion to strike the answer as not responsive and prejudicial, and further instructed the jury to disregard it. But the pearl had already dropped, beyond recall. The *ad hominem* maneuver, deftly used in court, is hard to offset, yet no brilliance is required for its use.

Q. When did you first see the defendant?
A. I believe it was June 3rd last.
Q. How do you fix the date?
A. I remember it because it was just a week after I lost my wife.

All the explosive objections of opposing counsel and all the admonitions of the court to the jury to forget the answer won't erase what the jury heard.

I recall a negligence case where my client, a pedestrian, sustained severe leg injuries when struck by the defendant's vehicle. Defense counsel was adept at making the honest witness look like an imposter. He noticed that the plaintiff looked at a paper in his pocket, and finally rose to the bait.

"May I see what you are looking at?"

My client pulled out the paper and handed it to defense counsel.

"What are these numbers written here? A code to the answers you're supposed to give?"

"No, sir. They are the plot and section numbers of my son's cemetery plot in Soldier's Cemetery. His body was just shipped back from Vietnam."

Saying the wrong thing for the right reason is no worse than saying the right thing for the wrong reason.

Pity the witness whose testimony an astute cross-examiner must refute or demolish, by whatever deceptive maneuver he can summon. It's akin to a lion stalking his prey, waiting for the right moment to make his kill. Counsel can be suave, almost deferential in his questioning, making his *who-not-what* points so bloodlessly the witness is unaware he is being skewered. Another will score his victories like claps of thunder.

The objective is the same in either case: destroy credibility. If your story is straightforward, with no gaps or inconsistencies, counsel still has *you*. And it is here that the *ad hominem* maneuvers abound.

It is unfortunate that justice is no more than an occasional by-product of the contest, with truth a rejected or invisible bystander because of the guile or bluff of trial counsel. After all, it is barely possible that an informer or stool pigeon is telling the truth, but at the hands of a skilled cross-examiner, with the ability of a F. Lee Bailey or Percy Foreman, his testimony can be twisted beyond recognition—not because of *what* was said, but because of *who* said it.

Yes, Virginia, trials are still showpieces, as little related to reality as the mirrored images on the walls of amusement parks, and *who-not-what* always plays a leading role.

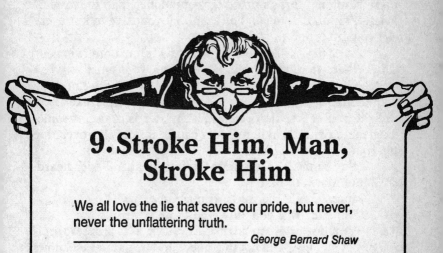

9. Stroke Him, Man, Stroke Him

We all love the lie that saves our pride, but never, never the unflattering truth.

———————————— *George Bernard Shaw*

Many people have complimented me. I am embarrassed, because I always feel they have not said enough.

———————————— *Oscar Wilde*

The Taste of Honey: Sweet to Sour   No part of the game of deception is beset with more pitfalls than compliments or flattery. Yet fewer gambits can more effectively prepare your listener to accept what you are about to offer him. Whatever maneuver you're planning, there's no better conditioner than the taste of honey. This doesn't mean, however, that you have to kiss every tush you are trying to condition.

Praise that is ill conceived or poorly framed can ruin your quest. When we receive a phony platitude, we instinctively wait for the other shoe to drop, sensing that the praise is but a prelude to something tricky that is sure to follow. Direct praise, like direct sunlight, can be uncomfortable. Much safer is praise of something the other *did,* rather than what he *is,* like this over-ripe sugarplum, for example:

"You're the best extemporaneous speaker I ever heard, bar none. The very best."

Much safer is the casual comment:

"I like the way you answered those criticisms."

To many, praise in any form is suspect. It arouses suspicion, if not anxiety. "I'm not that good, and he damn well knows it." Tolerance levels vary. Exceed them and you erect a subtle barrier.

The trick is to sense how your listener gets his verbal strokes. *What does he say or do that makes him feel good?* There lies the most fertile area for your blandishments.

Where the other is a braggart, or know-it-all, his need for reassurance gives him a higher tolerance level than the quiet and modest. Verbal stroking that strengthens his reassurance establishes an instant rapport. But pour it on so thick it moves from the obvious truth, and your friend will distrust you for telling him something he knows in his bones is not true. And that is no way to start your campaign. The most effective flattery is that which is pleasant but not too precise.

It helps in your manipulative quest if you correctly appraise the other. There is a breed that needs no prodding to give you a detailed tour of his life: his family, his church, his Rotary or job activities, and the demons that drive him on or turn him off.

Give him an admiring smile, a word of praise or envy, even

if you're drowning up to your eyeballs in the inordinate amount of crap he's pouring out. Be patient and you may topple barriers to believability in whatever manipulation you are attempting. But let him sense you-know-what and your efforts will collapse like a pricked balloon.

And most important, find or pretend to find some merit in whatever stance he assumes, no matter how infantile or irrelevant.

"You've a point there. I hadn't looked at it that way."

"There's a lot to what you say. I couldn't have said it better."

"No denying that, no siree."

Wait patiently for the appropriate moment to cut into the other's stream. To interrupt and drop your pearls prematurely might be considered as a half-baked judgment by you of what is being said. And that could blow your credibility. Deftly applied, a touch of flattery does the same thing to human nature that warmth does to a ball of wax.

Avoid negative verbal strokes, like:

"What did you do to your hair?"

"You're looking good, Tom. You put some weight on, I see."

"Congratulations. Hear you finally settled down."

"So you finally got here."

The dig is subtle, but unmistakable. You're giving a kiss and a kick at the same time. No less abrasive are the conditional strokes, which are best left unsaid.

"That's a good job done. But let's get on with it. There's a lot yet to be done."

"I like the project you started, even if it went over our budget. Try to stay in line in the future."

"Neat how you pulled that department out of the red. Think you can do it with the other units in your division? Their figures are pretty dismal, you know."

Unless you can deliver the stroke wholehearted, uncluttered with "ifs," "buts" and other qualifiers, forget it.

And never spray your strokes, like a fusillade of buckshot, hoping you'll be on target. Some of your compliments may be too

fulsome, others too patently phony for acceptance. The believable nugget could be lost in the maze, and even if recognized, lose
credibility in the garbage surrounding it.

> If power is the ultimate aphrodisiac, then deception by
> flattery is the climax *extraordinaire*.

Corporate manipulators jockeying for position or recognition
know the dangers in compliments that are too transparent. They
use a wide variety of deceptions to impress the chief executive,
avoiding always the accolade that is too fulsome or too
generalized.

It's no good, for example, to tell the boss he's "the greatest"
or the most productive manager in the entire outfit. Greatest in
what? Most productive of what?

Instead, dig up some of his more successful programs, a
few of the innovative ideas that struck pay dirt. And don't clobber
him with it. Pour it on too thick and it will resemble a dish of
Hollandaise sauce, beautiful to behold, but always on the verge of
curdling. Dress the compliment in modest garb; for example:

"Tom, I happened to look at that Empire Machine folder
last week, and the expansion we made into the Midwest territory.
At the bottom of the file, I saw your recommendation made a year
ago, when the project looked like a million-to-one shot. Had no
idea it was your brainchild. I wonder if you could give our division
a little talk on the criteria you used to formulate your recommendations?"

Carry your maneuvers a step further and dig into the
prejudices of your boss. What raises his hackles or turns him off
in company meetings or staff conferences? Are there any threats
to his position in the corporate organization, or barriers to his
promotion to a higher position? Then drop a nugget along these
lines:

"Somehow, I never did like Watson in our Monongahela
division. I don't know how you feel about him, but in my book he's
a first-class bastard, the way he cuts back on what we ship him.
And the garbage he throws out at our meetings!" Then, with a
long sigh, "If ever I met a pain in the you-know-where—."

You already know your thrust is mild compared to what
your listener thinks of Watson. You've flattered his judgment,

and that's a compliment of the first magnitude. What's more, you have shown yourself a good judge of character. Anyone can prove his good judgment by stating that's precisely what *you* have.

> If an animal is seen, felt, or heard by another that can exploit it in some way, a basis already exists for deception. . . . Strict neutrality does not exist in nature.[1]

The idea that platitudes can make another more susceptible to your manipulations is, of course, ridiculous—not just illogical or speculative, mind you, but totally ridiculous. Yet it works, more often than you imagine and in situations so varied that even Scheherazade, given another thousand and one nights, could not envision them.

Buried deep inside you is a reasonable facsimile of every man or woman you will ever attempt to manipulate, and the single most common frailty, a kind of inherited, genetic foolishness, is the love of praise.

"I dislike intensely the word 'manipulate,'" a teacher in the communicative arts told me. "It denotes using people by means of artifice and trickery. Like selling horseshit disguised as flattery. Somehow the image stinks."

"I agree. But the odor is so pervasive you no longer smell it," I replied. "It makes life one big game, whatever your role or goal. As often as not, your neighbor, friend, or competitor is ready, at the first opportunity, to better himself at your expense—subtly, as with faint praise, or more directly, even with a bloodletting maneuver, provided he can do it safely."

Basically, most of our relationships in the business or professional world are adversary in nature, some crude, most so subtle as to be barely recognizable. Your gain is another's loss, in a myriad of ways. When you raise yourself a niche higher than the other, it's usually at his expense.

The Cutting Edge of Praise

> Not that I love truth less
> But that I love success more
> —————————————— *Oscar Wilde*

"I agree, gentlemen, we should keep Barrows on the job. He's been with the company twenty-one years, is rarely absent, and has good health. True, he's brittle-tempered and has trouble keeping his department heads, but he's loyal. Can't deny that."

That's one way to skewer your friend. Much more effective than direct criticism and less a signal of how you feel about someone you never liked. You're not patently hostile, and this makes your criticism, couched in layers of faint praise, less self-serving.

Company politics employs a wide variety of deceptions to establish rank, or cut down threats to a position. Hatchet jobs are usually reserved for the upper hierarchy. Those below must rely on subtle maneuvers, camouflaged in flattery, or pretenses of long-standing friendship. Example:

"I like Jim. He's one helluva nice guy, real sharp most of the time, even though he has a genius for getting things screwed up."

"Bill did a good job on that Patterson deal, even though he has all the charm and wit of a wrong number. It makes up for all those mergers he conjured up last year."

"Why not send Terry on the job? I think he can close the deal for us. I'm confident he won't repeat the boners he pulled on the last one."

> And then I sigh, and with a piece of scripture, tell them that God bids us do good for evil. And thus I clothe my naked villainy, and seem a saint, when most I play the devil.[2]
> — *Shakespeare*

The cutting edge of praise can be honed to razor sharpness, making the incision almost bloodless. The gambits are not confined to corporate manipulations; for example:

A political analyst commented as follows on a New York TV program during the last Presidential primary campaign.

> Jimmy Carter is the most charismatic of the whole pack. He shows more leadership qualities, and makes a quick rapport with his audiences. Described by so many of his supporters as the one truly Christian and Christ reborn candidate, of which the South can be proud, he's a man to reckon with.

Praise indeed—in the boondocks of the deep South. But in New York City, a deft and lethal thrust.

Damning with faint praise can be polished to rapier-thrust effectiveness. But there are precautions to follow:

1. The praise should not be too fulsome, and must spring from the obvious, things generally known, more in the nature of reminders.

2. The thrust must be delivered casually, cushioned between layers of praise. I recall a correspondent describing an election in a banana republic in Central America, plagued with fears of Communist infiltration. Two contenders competed for a provincial office. One of the candidates, a wily character, distributed a circular a few days before the election, signed by an anonymous Committee of Interested Citizens and favoring the election of his opponent.

    But it was the kind of praise that packs a stiletto. It simply said that while this candidate once spoke favorably of Communism and the benefits to the province if it ever came there, he had since changed his mind and was now, the Committee believed, a sincere anti-Red. There wasn't enough time to repudiate the Committee. Besides, how do you go about denouncing a group that supports you?

3. Your cutting edge must be unbloodied by any trace of malice. This requirement can be a tough one. For example: a frequent trial opponent of mine was a formidable figure, with a talent for ridicule and a tongue sharp enough to cut glass. In a contested will contest, he cast himself in the role of underdog throughout the trial, using every trick to discredit and belittle. When he questioned a witness, his glare could open an oyster at twenty paces. In his closing remarks to the jury, he told them:

    "Now you will hear from Mr. Schweitzer, with his high-falutin language and fancy style. He'll play his usual violin of tears and sympathy. But don't let him fool you."

    It's your turn now. What do you tell the jury about your adversary? Praise him, even though he's been a first-class bastard throughout the trial. I replied:

    "My opponent is an able lawyer. Dedicated to his client, and an old friend of mine. When this case is over, we forget about it. What he says about me is good trial strategy. It works for him. Wins cases for him. It's his style.

I don't hold it against him, and I ask you not to. Never judge a client by his lawyer."

But they did, judging from the verdict.

When you just can't escape making a compliment, the reluctant but necessary kind, try hedging it. Like Alexander Woollcott's praise of Michael Arlen: "He's not as bad as they paint him. He's every other inch a gentleman." With a little practice you can learn how to lace almost any *bon mot* of flattery with a trace of arsenic. You may recall the politician who announced his support for Senator Muskie as President in 1968: "I'm for him 100%. I just want to prove you can beat somebody with a nobody."

Touch. Touch

> The principal object of flattery is "to flatten down, smooth, hence to *stroke* with the hand, caress."
>
> —————————————— *Oxford English Dictionary*
> *Vol. IV, p. 298*

So you have established a rapport of sorts, with a thread of compatibility linking you and your listener. Your remarks have shown you to be an excellent judge of character, ability, or whatever it was you praised so handsomely. The circumstances may even allow you to move into the arm-around-the shoulder stage, the confidential voice in the ear.

At this point you have a powerful tool at your disposal, a persuasive aid not fully appreciated. You have taken a giant step forward in whatever manipulation you have in mind.

A number of studies demonstrate that the skin receives and interprets a complex system of symbols and signals. It doesn't, in the words of one observer, "perform quite as well as the eye and ear in their specialized fields, but it is the *body's only receptor* that can communicate in both fields."

Ashley Montagu, in his classic work on the mind of the skin, points out the recognition accorded to its tactile functions. We "rub" people the wrong way, "stroke" them the right way. Someone has a "happy touch" or is a "soft touch." We "contact" people, or get "in touch" with them. Some are "thin skinned" or get "under one's skin." An experience deeply felt is "touching." Montagu aptly points out:

"It is strange that, although it is the skin, of all the organs of the body, that has most constantly occupied the forefront of man's consciousness, he should have paid little more than the most superficial attention to it."[3]

When we touch, we reach out for human contact, we affirm a personal relationship.

Pat someone on the shoulder, lay a hand on his arm, give him a hearty handshake, and you're saying: "I like you," "You're all right," "Everything is O.K." Hold her hand at the introduction a second or two longer, press it ever so slightly, and you have given her a signal not found in words.

Touching may have a limited power in the persuasion process, but it is dynamic. It's something you feel. It's tangible. It's a reaching out, a signal you like or are being liked. And more important, its meaning is crystal clear, unlike the nuances or subtleties that can shade what you are trying to say.

The thought that just touching an arm or shoulder of someone you know only casually will give you an assist in your manipulative quest is admittedly far-fetched—not absurd, just far-fetched, hardly to be imagined. But there it is, a carefully researched concept, not an abstract theory spawned in the brain of some academic crock.

A professor of psychology at the University of Connecticut, for example, concluded after a long study that even a fleeting touch will bring your listener a little closer to you. "A touch of less than a second has the power to make people feel better."[4]

So here you have a maneuver that will bring you closer to another, to dilute critical or hostile attitudes and establish a quick and warm rapport, regardless of the deception you're planning, whether a statistical trap or a put-on.

But it must come at the right moment, under the right circumstances, *and last no more than a few seconds* or it can turn into aggression. Only your instinctive awareness will give the answers; there are no ground rules or fixed guides.

As Flora Davis cautions: "Although most people enjoy being touched and respond well, whether they admit it to themselves or not, it takes a perceptive and sensitive person to know within the first few minutes with a stranger the right move at the right time."[5]

I remember hearing John McGraw, manager of the old New York Giants, relate how he tried to warm up to a sensational recruit from the Georgia boondocks. Obviously uneasy and suspicious, the lad stalled on signing a contract. The image of big-city slickers outfoxing a backwoods boy was an obvious obstacle to overcome. To soften the image, McGraw put his arm around the other's shoulder, as if to say: "Trust me, son."

It blew everything. "Don't try that father crap on me," the boy snapped and stalked from the room. A rival club got the deal.

But Don't Crowd   Space also communicates—loud and clear. What it says is simply this: *keep your distance.*

Get too close to your listener and you violate what Robert Ardrey calls "the Territorial Imperative," in his book by that name. He argues that we have an instinctive dislike for intrusions into our space zone, or what one psychologist describes as "the plastic bubble hovering over us." Ardrey contends that "the territorial nature of man is genetic and ineradicable." Although questioned by some behaviorists, his view has won growing acceptance.

Professor Edward Hall's extensive studies at Northwestern University on our personal space zones would appear to validate Ardrey's premise. Hall's conclusion: You impair your communicative ability by violating the compatible space area of your listener. Uneasiness grows to irritation and ends in dislike.

I heard a police official at the Buffalo, New York, headquarters warn detectives against crowding a suspect during his questioning. "You want him as relaxed as possible. The least hostility. Maybe he'll name others involved in the crime, or make admissions that will wrap up the investigation. There's a few safeguards that must be kept in mind, at all times. Never leave your side of the table. Get too close to the suspect and he'll feel threatened. I know from long experience that can blow everything."

At dinner recently with a psychologist, we discussed this book and behavior habits that impair effective persuasion. Conversation ran smoothly, until he gradually edged his chair closer and moved his water glass and ash tray to my side of the table. The movements were barely perceptible, but I found myself reaching for the ash tray to move it back across the table.

Finally he said: "You received a basic demonstration of nonverbal communication."

"What were you trying to communicate?" I asked.

"I made an aggressive move by entering your space zone. When we sat down we instinctively divided the table in half. I entered your half. No matter what I thereafter said to you, or how I said it, it would be filtered through your uneasiness. Our rapport was being slowly but surely broken. I couldn't sell you a ten spot for a single."

It sounded like the far-out jargon you find in academic journals. But later, during a trial in which I participated, I sensed a solid grain of truth in the point he was trying to make.

I stood a respectable distance from a witness during his preliminary cross-examination. I was polite, deferential. There was a rapport of sorts, as I led him into a series of contradictions and improbabilities. Then I moved closer, as if to reinforce the conversational tone of the questioning, finally resting an elbow on the edge of the witness box as I handed him several documents to examine. I sensed the witness's growing uneasiness. I was inside his space bubble. There was no room for him to retreat. He spoke more guardedly, weighing each answer, as if suddenly aware of the traps I was leading him into. The change was unmistakable.

My psychologist friend added a postscript to his observations: Your posture conveys a subtle message. Lean toward your listener and what you are saying carries a little more emphasis, more importance. But stay out of the other's space zone, unless you're in bed with your love mate, or packed in at a stand-up cocktail party. Which proves that crowding sometimes applies more to a feeling than physical space. What is crowding in a packed subway could be prized as intimacy in a discotheque.

10. The Manipulated Response

If you want someone to believe in a certain manner,
you must set the stage, and give him a cue.
_____ *Eric Hoffer*

He learned that sanity in a mad world was
disastrous, and wisdom counseled mimicry of the
disease for mutual reassurance.[1]
_____ *Francois Rabelais*

Impatient? Here you are at Chapter 10 of a book on the legitimate uses of deception and bluff, and you're probably asking: "Where and how do I begin?" Well, if you stayed with me from page 1, you could stop right here and justify what you paid for this book.

No magic formulas, true—no revolutionary ideas on the manipulation of your fellow man. And, besides, didn't Niccolo Machiavelli say all there was to be said on the subject, in his Florentine elegance? Not quite. It's one thing to state something, to make an observation, to philosophize on the frailties of the human species, and quite another to translate abstractions to specific suggestions, to give you handles you can grab and use (legitimately, of course) in everyday communication. Like the suggestions in this chapter for engineering a desired response.

The Baited Question   Not every question deserves a response. One of the brightest gems in McLuhan's bag of precepts on communication is his observation on listener participation: "Leave your message incomplete. Let your reader or viewer finish it and you've made him a part of it."

Consider these popular commercials:

"You can take Salem out of the country, but . . ."

"What spells relief from acid indigestion . . . ?"

A tricky manipulation of the response you want, much more effective than if spelled out and thrust upon the listener. It forces him to "hand-tailor" the message to fit himself, involves him subconsciously in whatever you're selling or offering— whether it's breakfast cereals, tires, stomach aids, or your friend's political candidacy. At least, that is the studied (and, I think, logical) conclusion of Dr. Herbert Krugman of General Electric, a knowledgeable researcher in consumer reaction.

The more unstructured your message, the more likely that the listener will try to fit himself into it. Most people don't like to admit they prefer answers supplied to them, which is why they so often receive a manipulated reply.

It's not too difficult to word what you're saying so that your listener becomes a participant. You can, by careful phrasing, make him unknowingly accept what you're offering, unaware that he has substituted your judgment for his. What he would have rejected if thrust upon him in complete form he may agree to simply because he completed the equation himself. The more you make him a part of it, the easier your quest.

Leave something, *anything*, to the imagination of the other if you think it will help engineer the response you want.

> When people agree, it is only in their conclusions; their reasons are always different.
> ———————————————— *George Santayana*

Forty years' experience in the trial courts has shown me repeatedly how suggestible an animal is man. Lawyers know instinctively that using the "yes" or positive factor short-circuits reason and inhibits a critical evaluation of what is being said.

Properly framed, a question can be a tool of deception, by strongly suggesting the desired answer and giving it a good dose of credibility at the same time.

"If you can't trust Dr. Jones to handle this situation, who can you trust?"

"Why are people paying a little more to get a Zenith?"

"I don't have to tell you what happened after that, do I?"

How much more arresting than the bare statement "More people are buying Zenith to get better value" or "I think Dr. Jones can handle this situation"! And with a little manipulation and skullduggery you can sharpen the cutting edge of your question:

"Is the great state of California finally ready to select a candidate that is this honest and forthright?"

"Is our city ready for a mayor who is hard on crime, fearless, and incorruptible?"

Subtle, yet biting. More effective than a frontal assault of calling your opponent dishonest, less than forthright, or soft on crime.

A simple question, properly framed, can also be the cutting edge in creating doubt or uncertainly concerning a proposition you want destroyed.

"How in the wide world could any thinking person accept that suggestion?"

"Now tell me, honestly, have you in all your years heard anything more ridiculous?"

I heard a political candidate at a large meeting tick off a list of criticisms of his opponent, ending each, after a dramatic pause, with the same query: "Is this the man you're going to elect to this high office?" A thunderous "no" was the manipulated response each time. Listener involvement at its best.

Eric Hoffer said it well: "There is a powerful craving in most of us to see ourselves as instruments in the hands of others and thus free ourselves from the responsibility for acts which are prompted by our own questionable inclinations and impulses. Both the strong and the weak grasp at the alibi."[2]

There is little doubt that a "no" response at the start creates a difficult barrier to overcome. Pride demands that this negative stance be continued. Once a person has responded "no," a change would tend to diminish worth. As Dr. Harry Overstreet comments in his perceptive work *Influencing Human Behavior:* "Get someone to answer 'no' at the beginning, and it takes the wisdom and patience of angels to transform that bristling negative into an affirmative."

So aim for positive answers at the outset, stroking wherever possible, and framing your question to implant belief or disbelief in whatever proposition you're proposing or opposing. This Socratic tactic of deception and cajolery may:

1. Provoke a positive response to your remarks, or at least
2. Draw out your listener so you will know by his answer what imprint you've made so far, or
3. Suggest the absurdity of any alternative to what you're suggesting.

Don't try to moralize on these ploys. You should have learned by now that it's futile to judge a deception by its motive. Deception can be its own motive.

The Assumed Reply   The response you want can be a direct affirmation, clear and unequivocal. If that's not possible, try coming in the back door. Simply assume the answer you want has already been given. Then frame a query based on that assumption.

Make it an innocent question, disarming in its simplicity—never argumentative, never accusatory. Unless the reply flatly repudiates your assumption, you've manipulated the other into giving the response you want. He's locked in tight. This is a favorite gambit of trial lawyers, but its use is by no means confined to the courtroom. For example:

"Let's consider now this mistake of the Pentagon in timing the promotion of the MIRV's. Do you think it made any difference in our present detente with Russia?" Whether the answer is "yes" or "no," it concedes your major premise, that a mistake *was* made.

"In view of his compromise of artistic standards, do you think he should wait a few months before his next show?" An answer either way admits the compromise.

More subtle: "Sure, you can live without wine, but how well?"

The Manipulated Witness   Now see how lawyers employ the manipulated-response maneuver. You may not be a lawyer and may never conduct a cross-examination in court, but you can learn much by observing how trial counsel strokes a witness to elicit the responses he wants. The tactic obviously won't endear him to whomever he entraps, any more than your ploy will endear you to whomever you've manipulated to deliver the "right" answer, when awareness of your deception dawns.

A skilled cross-examiner will condition a witness during the preliminary phases of questioning by eliciting "yes" responses to simple and innocuous queries in order to disarm him for the thrusts to follow. F. Lee Bailey tells lawyers at trial seminars: "You peel the onion layer by layer. You don't begin by stabbing for the heart."

> To appear the friend of man, when in reality we are no longer so, is to reserve to ourselves the means of doing him an injury by surprising honest men into an error.
> ——————————————————— *Edmund Rostand*

Cross-examination, not unlike seduction, usually begins with a stroking ritual, a stratagem you can always use to good advantage. Counsel knows that an initial display of aggressiveness will stiffen the witness, put him on guard. He knows also that, as in lovemaking, you don't jump to the main course for the simple reason you won't enjoy the main event to the fullest if you don't pause at the hors d'oeuvres.

A series of harmless questions sets the mood. They smooth relationships, drain hostility, much like the opening gambit in a conversation:

"Hi! Everything O.K.?"

"Just fine."

"You're looking good."

"Feeling fine."

Disarming. Harmless. But a put-on. In cross-examination, the stroking game is often a prelude to disaster. The rapier thrust is made swiftly, smoothly, skewering the witness before he's aware of what happened.

Q. You were walking down Main Street?

A. I was.

Q. Talking to your wife?

A. Yes.

Q. And minding your own business?

A. Of course.

Q. When a loud crash at the corner drew your attention in that direction?

A. That's correct.

Obviously all that preceded the crash was not seen by the witness. Even if he did get a glimpse of the impact a moment before it happened, or the speed and course of the cars, his testimony is already watered down. It must have been what he imagined happened, or what his lawyer told him happened. No amount of explanation will remove the sting of his inadvertent admission.

So beware of the master of the manipulated response, the unctuous cross-examiner, the let's-be-friends type. He disarms you at the outset by a clever, yet simple stratagem of asking questions that are merely rehashes of those you've already answered on direct examination, the kind that call for no more than a "Yes, that's right" reply.

Straightforward, simplistic, no hidden traps. Your confidence mounts, tensions relax. This friendly examiner is different from what you expected. He wants the truth, and by God, he's going to get it.

But it will be his version, given in the way he wants it given.

Actually, you're being readied for a classic verbal rape. You won't feel the initial thrust. It will be utterly painless. Before you realize it, you've agreed to something you never intended. You try to explain, to shade your answer, shift the emphasis, but the more you talk, the deeper you sink, until you're up to your ears in contradictions. Suddenly this friendly character has turned into a first-class bastard. He's put you on a limb and sawed it off.

And that, my good friend, is a classic example of the engineered answer.

11. That Beautiful Man of Straw

Xenophon shows in his *Life of Cyrus* the necessity of deception to success: the first expedition of Cyrus against the king of Armenia is replete with fraud, and it was deceit alone, and not force that enabled him to seize that kingdom. And Xenophon draws no other conclusion from it than that a prince who wishes to achieve great things must learn to deceive.

———————————————— *Machiavelli*

I do not mean to suggest that the custom of lying has suffered any decay of interruption—no, for the Lie, as a Virtue, a Principle, is eternal; the Lie, as a recreation, a solace, a refuge in time of need, the fourth Grace, the tenth Muse, man's best and surest friend, is immortal, and cannot perish from the earth. . . . My complaint simply concerns the decay of the art of lying. No high-minded man, no man of right feeling, can contemplate the lumbering and slovenly lying of the present day without grieving to see a noble art so prostituted.[1]

———————————————— *Mark Twain*

A Man for All Seasons

> Today, and probably since Adam first laid eyes on Eve,
> ethics stretches to fit need.

Build a straw man, wherever and whenever you can—if it serves your purpose. It's an ancient tactic, deeply imbedded in the human psyche.

The Jews, for centuries, served as straw men for rulers plagued by economic woes or for religious zealots determined to increase their flock. Blacks were pictured as a menacing tide by Southern aristocrats at the turn of the century. The Reds are a perennial favorite in countries where the military lusts for power, or where the power manipulators have learned that a climate of fear of the Communists will bring fat contracts for war material. Then there was the Yellow Peril and the rising tide of Roman Catholicism in the late nineteenth century—all beautiful men of straw. Few maneuvers of deception wear so innocuous a mask or are so commonplace and socially acceptable. Deeply buried in the human psyche is the drive to avoid culpability by shifting blame to another. The "other" can be real or a myth. One is as easily made credible as the other.

> The bluff is not only as American as apple pie; it's certain to
> be a la mode for many years to come.
> —————————————————— *Henry L. Mencken*

I recall a directors' meeting where some concern was voiced about the mounting number of customer complaints of delays in receiving the merchandise ordered. The division manager was summoned for an explanation.

He could not, without endangering his own position, point to his lack of control of key personnel, or his poor judgment in selecting department heads.

"The delays are indeed unfortunate," he explained. "The carriers we used for our interstate hauling have been plagued for some time by a quiet slowdown among their drivers and dispatchers. This unpublicized strike reached its peak just about the time these losses were incurred. Unfortunately, neither the companies nor the unions will admit to its existence, but the situation has been remedied. I anticipate no more delays."

He buried the mythical slowdown in a fog of words, adroitly contrived to create a man of straw.

"I will not yield on these budget items. They can criticize me all they want. Their threats won't move me one iota."

What threats? What criticism? That they are pure fantasy won't diminish the image of courage they create.

"I ask you, gentlemen, to consider my appointment strictly on the merits, and not listen to the insinuations that I am a Communist. You know me long enough to know how untrue these innuendos are."

Beautiful and effective, even if no such insinuations were ever made. The straw man clouds the fact that the speaker is totally unsuited to the position he seeks.

From an address before a military group by a candidate for the U.S. Senate:

"You know who these Congressional stonethrowers are, who seek every chance to get on TV and radio, so they can demean our servicemen. . . . Their critical remarks are aimed at discrediting our servicemen, destroying their morale, and making a military career something to be ashamed of."

There were no stonethrowers, no criticisms of the military. But the ploy established a quick and solid rapport with the audience.

Statesmen and politicians make straw men like Carvel makes ice cream. The dragon they belabor is always the mythical "they." This casts them in the mould of a heroic David pitted against an army of Goliaths.

Deception is never so successful as when she baits her hook with a persuasive myth.

"I don't care how hard they try to smear my personal life—and God knows, they've tried awfully hard. There's not a single thing they can point to."

"They're playing a vicious game, trying with these rumors to link me with the underworld. You've known me and my family long enough to discredit these rumors."

"They." "They." "They." Dragonlike figures of the first magnitude, beyond immediate comprehension. Ghostly, yet powerful. This faceless source has a variety of pseudonyms.

Grapevine. Strong rumor. Gossip. Good authority. Take your pick, but be careful to keep it vague and indefinite. Hinting at a specific source, or even implying its existence, could rob your straw man of credibility.

There are four simple guidelines to bear in mind in using this maneuver:

1. Select a straw man that meets the test of plausibility. It must not be so conjectural as to strain credulity. While myths sorely need some trace of credibility—not necessarily truths—they need not be married to logic. Myths not only disagree with truths, they often quarrel among themselves.
2. Build it up, using no more than bare suggestion or innuendo.
3. The stratagem must be beyond ready detection or quick exposure.
4. If you are the deceivee, never chase something you suspect is a deception, built on a straw man. Let it alone and in time it may talk itself to death.

Straw Men in Court   You can shape a workable strategy by observing how lawyers—those masters at deception—use straw men in watering down the culpability of their client.

> They have no lawyers among them, for they consider them a sort of people whose profession it is to disguise matters.
> ———————————————— *Sir Thomas More*

There is an unwritten rule almost instinctively followed by defense counsel in a criminal case: Build a man of straw as soon as you can, the sooner the better. There is no more effective stratagem to win an acquittal or sow the seeds of reasonable doubt.

There was a period, for example, when the Vietnam war gave defense counsel an opportunity to put society on trial if his client was a battle veteran of that conflict.

I recall a robbery trial in Buffalo, New York, where the holdup victim was brutally and needlessly beaten. The defense predictably claimed that the country was at fault in the monster it created. When the jury retired to deliberate its verdict, all but one juror voted for conviction. I later learned that this juror, himself a veteran, argued at length that the war machine, by training the defendant to kill, destroyed conscience and compassion.

"It would be inhuman to hold this boy responsible for doing what he was taught and compelled to do." A convenient straw man. The other jurors finally agreed and voted a "Not Guilty" verdict.

It is a time-honored gambit for defense counsel to put the victim on trial. In the trial of Candy Mossler for the death of her husband, the victim's background proved more important to the jury than the guilt or innocence of the defendant.

Simply to deny that your client committed the crime is never as exculpatory as offering a possible alternative. It need not be provable, or even logical. It can be no more than suggestive, with only a trace of plausibility, as long as it supplies an answer to the question *If the defendant didn't do it, who did?*

In the Candy Mossler trial, Percy Foreman, the brilliant and legendary lawyer, lost no time in his opening address in planting the seeds of his defense:

"Distinguished gentlemen of the prosecution and your honor, the court, gentlemen of the jury and alternates," he saluted his audience, "we believe the evidence in this case suggests that if each of the thirty-nine wounds inflicted on Jacques Mossler on the early morning of June 30, 1964, had been done by a different person, that is, by thirty-nine different people, there would still be at least three times that many people in Florida and the Mossler empire with either real or imaginary justification to want the death of Jacques Mossler."[2]

Foreman continued, describing the decedent as a sexual deviate, a swinger who, not content with his homosexual partners, would pick up strangers to indulge his sexual fantasies. "His appetites ran to masochism, sadism, voyeurism, and all the perversions mentioned in *Psychopathia Sexualis,* Krafft-Ebing's great masterpiece. He would approach high-school students and college boys . . . in bars frequented by the gay people." Counsel stressed that the savagery of this killing was typical of enraged sexual deviates.

No proof whatever was offered to substantiate these accusations, not a single witness was called to admit homosexual acts with Mossler or testify he had seen the decedent engage in homosexual activity. But that was not the only supposition Foreman offered, while he wisely decided to make no serious effort to meet the state's case against his client.

He charged that the deceased destroyed uncounted businessmen with his devious dealings and on occasion hired underworld thugs to rid him of blackmailers. "Jacques Mossler was ruthless in business as any pirate who ever sailed the seas of commerce." There were, Foreman charged, many men within his own organization that stood to profit by his death.

Beautiful straw men. And so they remained for the duration of the trail. *Not one of these charges proven, not even a pretense at establishing their truth.* There was, of course, no obligation on the defense to prove anything. The burden of proof remained with the prosecution. The defense could, however, legitimately bring to the attention of the jury whatever made the state's case less credible, in this instance a claim that other persons had a strong and compelling motive for killing Mossler—a premise that the jury, by its verdict of acquittal, fully accepted.

The district attorney spent most of his summation in attacking the defense tactics.

"It is an old technique—as old as criminal law itself—to put the victim on trial for a murder case," he said. "The defense has had highly skilled lawyers with unlimited funds to divert your attention from the guilt of Candace Mossler and her nephew. Who will stand up and speak for the murdered man?" He then proceeded to do so. He claimed that greed and lust had led Candy and Mel to murder Mossler, and that they were stooping to disgusting depths in accusing the victim of homosexuality. "Mossler's only crime," he said, "was getting in the way of the love affair."

But his pleas fell on deaf ears.

Deception begins by making a falsehood look like truth and ends by making truth appear like falsehood.

I plead guilty—reluctantly—to use of the same tactic, as must all defense counsel, in varying degrees.

I represented a young man in Buffalo, New York, accused of rape. There were serious doubts in my mind as to the identification of the defendant. My cross-examination of the complainant proceeded along these lines:

Q. Did you tell the police at any time you were not sure they had the right man?
A. I did not.
Q. And that you thought the man that raped you was taller?
A. That's not true.
Q. With reddish hair?
A. I never said that.
Q. Or that he spoke with a slight accent?
A. Not true.
Q. Then why did you make the statement to the police at the line-up: "I only wish I was more sure?"
A. I never did.

All the denials of the complainant, all the angry denunciations of this tactic by the prosecutor in his closing remarks to the jury, did not erase the possibility (in my own mind a certainty) that the identification was in error. True or not, a man of straw had suddenly appeared on the scene, creating enough doubt in the minds of some of the jurors to result in a deadlock. My client unfortunately died before the retrial.

Earl Rogers, the legendary criminal lawyer, represented a policeman accused of a brutal and unprovoked assault. He subpoenaed a number of the defendant's fellow officers, and asked each a single question:

"Isn't it true that the complaining witness has a twin brother who resembles him greatly and that this twin brother is a notorious crook for whom the police have been looking?"

The prosecutor sprang to his feet with a heated objection. The court sustained the objection and roundly criticized Rogers for his maneuver. Rogers bowed to the judge with his customary gravity and abruptly rested his case. The defense, relying on the straw man it had created, presented no other witnesses. An acquittal followed. The jury found it hard to believe that the complaining witness did not actually have a twin brother who was a fugitive from justice.

12. The Illusion of Relevancy

Gratiano speaks an infinite deal of nothing. . . . His reasons are as two grains of wheat hid in two bushels of chaff; you shall seek all day ere you find them, and when you have them, they are not worth the search.[1]

—————————————————————— *Shakespeare*

I believe because it is absurd.

—————————————————————— *Tertullian*

The Wrong Side of Logic

Errours, Like Straws upon the surface flow;
Who would search for Pearls must dive below.[2]
———————————————————————— *John Dryden*

A revered French philosopher, René Descartes, wrote over 300 years ago in his classic work *Discourse on Method* that good thinking and sound action rest on four basic precepts:

a. To avoid prejudice
b. To avoid offering as true what you do not clearly know to be true.
c. To avoid discussing the complex until you have first explained the things that are simplest and easiest to understand.
d. To offer the whole, omitting nothing.

But this was in 1637. The character and style of our present times compel a new set of ground rules. To compete successfully today, it *may* be necessary:

a. To induce others to accept as true matters which on close or more rational examination they might find unacceptable.
b. To blur differences and distinctions.
c. To make the simple look complex and the complex simple.
d. To make the speculative look authoritative.

These, in a nutshell, are the sinews of deception and bluff. If you find these ingredients unpalatable, skip this chapter.

> You score, not by what you have actually proved, or say you have proved, but what you make the other *think* you have proved.

———————————————————————————————————

If people's minds were empty to start with, you could more readily do your inplanting. But they are not empty. They are full of opinions, prejudices, likes and dislikes; some of them putty-soft and nebulous, easy to push aside, some hard as concrete. And the logic commonly employed to persuade would make Aristotle turn in his grave. Listen carefully to political pronouncements or everyday conversations, and you'll find fallacies dropping like snow in January.

The study of logic in textbooks and college courses is unfortunately buried in a quagmire of theoretical confusion. In political analysis, for example, out of the vast sea of literature on the subject I found only one work that deals frankly with harsh realities: Machiavelli's *The Prince*. It is effective because it is practical, and it is practical because it is keyed to basic weaknesses in human nature, and thereby demonstrates the power of illusion over reality.

Compare this work, for example, with Aristotle's *Politics* or Hobbes' *Leviathan*, two heavies in college courses, and it shines like a beacon in the murky darkness.

A long-time student of logic, I once tried to compile a table of fallacies in common use. The list grew endless, with each author using his own terminology. There was no uniformity, not even in the Latin terms traditionally used to describe mutations of logic and syllogistic fallacies. One college textbook showed a list of twenty-one, another thirty-six. Stuart Chase's description of thirteen types of false reasoning comes closest to a practical discussion of the syllogistic fallacies commonly encountered.

Unfortunately, this outpouring of creativity gives no handles to grab in our everyday experience.

The handles I describe in this book will offend some of my readers, amuse others. You may not choose ever to use them. But at least you will be able to recognize them. And in recognizing them, you will have gained some insight into their use in your everyday life and a measure of protection the next time someone tries to ready you for a verbal seduction.

Analogies Spin the Web   So you want to prove a point. You fish around for a good persuader. Look for a simple analogy. Something you can use in place of proof—even if it's on the wrong side of logic.

For example, a New York newspaper carried a reader's letter decrying reliance by Canada upon its projected wall of radar. "It won't stop enemy bombers. Look at the Great Wall of China. Look at the Maginot Line. The only true defense is a good defense. Hit them first."

Persuasive? Of course, if you read while you run. What does a stone wall have in common with electronic detectors? Only the word "wall," no more.[3]

Said a reader's letter to a London newspaper:

> England was troubled the most during the past fifty years by men who had one basic similarity: their names have six letters and ended in the same two letters. Kaiser, Kruger, Hitler and Nasser. Are we being told something?

Yes, of course: that the writer is a nut of the first dimension. But before you laugh it off, read some of the letters-to-the-editor in your own daily. Not as far-out as the above, perhaps, but just as loose in their use of analogies to spin illusions of relevancy.

If America continues to build nuclear bomb deterrents, she will be safe from attack.

We will not build any more nuclear bomb deterrents.

Therefore America will not be safe from attack.

You can dress up this type of syllogistic fallacy in a fog of words and phrases, masking it beyond easy recognition.

Students who studied diligently passed the examination.

Tom passed the examination.

Therefore Tom studied diligently.

It's not too difficult to shape an analogy into a tool of deception. Simply remember these basic precepts:

1. Two or more things are analogous when they appear similar in one or more respects. The more points of similarity you can offer, the stronger your analogy.
2. The similarities must have a plausible, or at least a superficially plausible, relationship to each other.

3. If your main premise is beyond the experience of your listener, contrive an analogy that explains it by comparison with things within his experience. Bluff and deceptions, like poisons, will usually be rejected when administered alone, but when laced with a modicum of truth, may be swallowed undetected.

4. Analogies with a subjective appeal are always more persuasive than those which call for an objective approach. In the former, you make your listener feel that it would be to his advantage if what you're saying is true; that the analogy *must* be true for that reason. Objective thinking is coldly analytical. A good trial lawyer knows instinctively "the heart hath reasons the mind will never know."

I recall the deadly effectiveness with which one of our two living ex-Presidents used false analogies in his campaign for re-election:

My opponent sounds more and more like a communist sympathizer. He bitterly opposes measures to build our armed forces to No. 1 strength. It will cost too much. This is precisely what Moscow wants to hear.

Sharply toned, to be sure, and the acme in deception. But no less deceptive than the oft-repeated analogy between the thirteen American colonies in 1787 and the efforts after the last war to establish a strong World Constitution. "If they were able to compose their differences and adopt a constitution, why can't the quarreling nations get together?"

A good analogy? Hardly. The American colonies had a single language, a single culture, one Christian religion, and a single, compact location.

A public official was asked how he managed to build a $200,000 home and acquire $250,000 in bonds, after serving twenty years in office on a modest salary. "Just look around you," he replied. "Compare me to thousands of other Americans who by frugality and hard work, raised themselves from poverty to a level not much different from mine." Yes, but on a salary of $12,000 a year?

More subtle is the analogy drawn by President Nixon

between poverty and relief: "You can't cure poverty by throwing money at it."

The New York Times demolished this logic in an editorial:

"Let us suppose a man is drowning thirty feet from shore. A rescuer throws him ten feet of rope. He drowns. It would scarcely be logical to conclude: 'Rope is of no use in the prevention of drowning.'

"Yet that is the kind of logic enshrined in President Nixon's budget and set forth in his radio talk. The President blandly asserts that the Federal programs enacted in the last decade were based on the assumption that any human problem could be solved simply by throwing enough Federal dollars at it.

"There was no such assumption and no such flood."

Proof by analogy is deeply embedded in our thinking processes. Similarities offer a seductive lure: because two things resemble each other, or have a casual connection of sorts, they are intimately related. Analogies convince or persuade in a wholly irrational manner.

The trick, of course, if you can bury your scruples, is to contrive an analogy plausible enough to take the place of proof and strong enough to replace common sense with the blurred vision of prejudice, bigotry, or whatever best serves the deception you have in mind.

And don't forget the innuendo, that precious gem of deception. In his memoirs, Richard Nixon wrote that "No White House in history could have survived the kind of operation Archibald Cox was planning," reminding us that Cox was not just a Democrat and Harvard professor, but *a friend of the Kennedys*. And any simpleton knows that a friend of the Kennedys is incapable of conducting a fair investigation.

This-Must-Follow-That

> Those things which are most real are the illusions I create.
> ———————————————————————— *Delacroix*

Aristotle was the first to describe a syllogism and the verbal manipulations it makes possible. A syllogism (simplified by Stuart Chase in his excellent work *Guide to Straight Thinking*) is a combination of these propositions: a major premise, a minor premise, and a conclusion.

> Harvard Law graduates make superior lawyers. John Smith graduated Harvard Law School. Therefore John Smith is a superior lawyer.

___

When two conditions exist side by side, we are impelled to assume that one explains or is related to the other (*post hoc, propter hoc*—this must follow that). Verbal manipulators in all walks of life exploit this faulty logic.

George Bernard Shaw was both a brilliant playwright and a vegetarian. *Ergo:* there must be some relationship between that type of diet and mental agility.

> The American Communist favors arms reduction. Senator Jones favors arms reduction. Therefore Senator Jones is a Communist.

___

The streets of Philadelphia were reported in *Newsweek* as "looking cleaner and better repaired" after Mayor Rizzo took office than during the prior administration. True, but not because of the good Mayor. A reader wrote to the editor: "In 1972–1973, there was, for the first time, absolutely no snow or freezing rain in Philadelphia. Thus, the potholes and other damage caused by normal winter weather did not appear."[4]

The first step is to persuade your listener or reader to accept a given premise or statement as the truth; once this is done, you can spin from it a myriad of conclusions, depending on the manipulations you have in mind. *But there must be a thread of plausibility to the conclusions.*

"The air in New York City is heavily polluted, about the worst in the nation."

Arguable, but assuming acceptance of this premise, don't try forcing the conclusion that:

"Residents in the Big Apple have a 20 year shorter life span than those living in Casper, Wyoming."

This lacks even a thin thread of plausibility. Much more palatable is the observation: "There are more respiratory problems in New York City than in less polluted areas of the nation."

It is in the grey areas, where plausibility merges with absurdity, that deception flourishes.

The fallacy of *post hoc, propter hoc* is particularly flattering to doctors. They prescribe for symptoms that eventually disappear. The fact that the recovery might be due entirely to the patient's natural recuperative powers is overlooked. Also overlooked is that many cures or improvements in health are not due to medical treatment, but simply to improved standards of living—better nutrition, water, sanitation, and housing.

One thing so obviously follows another, there *must* be a connection. Here you have one of the most common devices for creating illusions of relevancy. It abounds everywhere, hidden in gobbledygook, doubletalk, campaign oratory, and pronouncements from Washington.

Try "this-must-follow-that" to prove a proposition not otherwise provable. It's not too difficult a maneuver, and once mastered, it becomes a powerful tool of deception.

Talking in Circles   To effectively argue in circles, start with a proposition that is not too implausible. The rest is comparatively easy. "Although there is no proof, there is no disproof."

"The New Testament is infallible. Absolutely."

"Why so?"

"Because The Book was inspired by God and speaks His word. Nowhere else does He speak to man."

"How do you know that?"

"It says so in The Book, doesn't it?"

Myself when young did eagerly frequent
Doctor and Saint, and heard great argument
About it and About: but evermore
Came out by the same door where in I went.[5]
————————————————— *Edward Fitzgerald*

The leader of a religious sect claims that no true believer ever suffers an illness, even slight.

"But I know that some of your followers have been ill," a skeptic points out.

"That's because they were not true believers."

"How can you prove that?"

"They got sick, didn't they?"

You can argue that "men's suits made in Scotland are the best wearing anywhere in the world."

"How can you prove that?"

"Simple. They're made of Scottish wool, aren't they?"

You're on the same level as a child's answer to the question "Why are you doing that?"

The one word reply: "Because."

Oscar Wilde remarked that all mankind, excepting himself, of course, was "utterly stupid." Challenged for the basis of his opinion, he replied: "You disagree with me. What more proof do you want?"

Arguing in a circle, *circulus in probando,* is a familiar device that tries to prove the unprovable. Listen carefully to some arguments, and you'll find that the speaker is saying no more than: "It's true because I say it's true." It's much like a lawyer telling the jury in his summation: "I submit these, ladies and gentlemen, as the conclusions upon which I base my facts."

Even if not in so many words, this is a common ploy of trial counsel and the professional witness to make the incredible credible. The maneuver is so deeply ingrained, it is practiced subconsciously.

A doctor, sued for malpractice, claims his treatment was proper.

"How do you know your treatment was proper?"

"I should know. I wrote a textbook describing this disease and its treatment."

"How do you know that the book is accurate?"

"I wrote it, didn't I?"

Granted, this is too obvious a crock of manure. Illusions of relevancy are more clearly constructed—since the constructors are generally clever people. But not all.

A visitor asked a mental patient why he continually snapped his fingers. "It scares away tigers in the area."

"That's absurd. There's no tigers within 5,000 miles of here."

"You're right. Works, doesn't it?"

Arguing in a circle is calculated deception, making a pretense of proving something but actually doing no more than repeating in different form what you are trying to establish.

With a little practice, you can learn how to use a conclusion to prove itself. Follow these simple rules:

1. Your major premise must be lacking in logical proof. If what you seek to establish can be proven by reasonable argument, forget *circulus in probando*.
2. State your conclusion.
3. Now disguise it by rewording, rephrasing.
4. Cite No. 3 as proof of No. 2.

The Anemic Conclusion　　Never express your conclusion edged with doubt or uncertainty. Learn the difference between a strong and an anemic conclusion. The following, for example, are flaccid and pedestrian, to be avoided:

Suggests that . . .
Indicates that . . .
Probably is true that . . .
You can fairly deduce that . . .
Points to the conclusion that . . .
Seems to bear out my point . . .

Regardless of the strength or weakness of your premise, if it bears any semblance of plausibility, play from strength.

You have to conclude that . . .
It proves beyond any reasonable doubt . . .
How can you possibly avoid the conclusion that . . .
From which it follows, as night follows day, that . . .
We can be certain that . . .

It's the difference between saying: "It doesn't appear to be true" and "It's just not true."

The Over-Generalization   This is the most easily learned maneuver. It's childishly absurd, yet as pervasive as weeds in a grassy patch. And it works. You can apply it in support of a wide variety of conclusions, ranging from the preposterous to the plausible. I sit as a magistrate in a small Western town where the ranch and farm hands include a good number of Mexicans. A state legislator opposed appointment of a Mexican to a supervisory position.

"You simply can't trust them. You should know. You're a judge there. Look at the high percentage of crimes they commit, in prison they far outnumber the others, and there's the problem of communication."

"But this man is college trained," I pointed out. "Never committed a crime, speaks English as fluently as you or I."

He failed to get the appointment. His name and looks were too Mexican, although he is an American citizen. He was generalized out of a job he deserved. Look around you and see how this manipulation has become a convenient tool of deception and exaggeration. It's the basic ingredient in jokes, epigrams, cartoons, advertisements, and alarmist predictions by politicians.

Relevant to What?   A shotgun sprays, but the rifle bores deep. So with your quest at persuasion or deception: fix your objective with precision, know precisely what proposition you want to make credible, and then direct your analogies, syllogisms, or whatever tactic is appropriate to that target.

So many attempts at persuasion die stillborn. They are beautifully presented, yet result in no more impact than a baby's touch. They simple don't catch fire. The listener is unmoved or bored and shows it by his yawns or frequent interruptions.

Untouched in the thicket of your remarks is the decisive factor that cuts clean and deep in shaping opinion. As one astute trial lawyer put it: "Get lost in the chicken shit and you've lost your listener."

But don't shoot for the bullseye until you have fixed it clear and firm in your sights. A blunderbuss attack usually results in a half-assed presentation. There's no sense leading a cavalry charge when a single rapier thrust will do the job—quicker and better.

Beware lest you lose the substance by grasping at the
shadows.

—————————————————————————————— *Aesop*

Once you have spotted the jugular, decide on the maneuvers you
will use and then set your course without delay. Some would-be
manipulators are as slow in coming about as a square-rigger in a
flat calm. A few, experienced in word duelling, such as lecturers,
lawyers, or semanticists, have developed an instinct for spotting
the nitty-gritty of a presentation and knowing when to grab for it,
like surfers who know instinctively when to catch the curl of the
wave.

Gobbledygook flourishes in conversation no less than in
legal documents or political speeches. George Ade, the venerable
humorist, was half right, when he observed that "for parlor use
the vague generality is a lifesaver, but for persuasion, it is sound
without substance."

Most persuaders aspiring to a verbal rape just muddle
through, trying mentally to separate the wheat from the chaff
and then using the chaff.

Ideally, your objective is to minimize differences, stress
agreements, and narrow the point at issue. You'll accomplish this
quicker if, at the outset, you crystallize in your mind what specifi-
cally you want your listener to accept. Fuzzy thinking will cause
you to grope blindly, spouting an avalanche of words in the hope
your outpouring will somehow accomplish the seduction.

13. The Weight of Ethos

Man is a gregarious animal, and much more so in his mind than his body. He may like to go alone for a walk, but he hates to stand alone in his opinions.

——————————————— *George Santayana*

Everybody knows it.
Any thinking person will tell you
Surveys prove it beyond a doubt
Nine out of ten people will tell you
Laboratory tests have proven
The Bible says it over and over
Did you know this was Napoleon's favorite brandy?

_____

If you can seduce your listener to believe that admired figures, accepted authorities, or the "in people" are saying the same things you are, you've injected a good dose of credibility into whatever you're offering. "It's got to be good. The astronauts used it, didn't they?"

Ad verecundian (appeal to a higher and reversed authority) can be manipulated into a tool of deception, stirring the emotions, blurring reason. I recall a newspaper cartoon showing a group of elderly matrons at a social tea, one of them saying: "I was never sure what to think until I heard Eric Severeid. Now, with him retired, I don't know what or who to believe."

While you can't beat the Bible or Constitution as persuaders, you can score with almost any attribution you make, provided it points to a respected source. It's a human frailty to revere the quoted opinions of higher-ups, true or untrue. We instinctively defer to the opinions of "authorities," pseudo or real.

Proof based on ethos or "they can't all be wrong" reasoning, is a widely used bait; if you carefully analyze it, you'll find most of it a mix of half-truths, no truths, or exaggerations.

Obviously the more general the authorities or sources you select, the safer you are against detection. How would you go about disproving that a specific product contains more of the ingredients recommended by doctors than any other on the market? Or that a named cereal is eaten by more athletes than any other?

You don't confine your ethos proof to specific authorities. You let it ride on subtle innuendoes or references, carefully planned to create an impression of high moral worth or universal approval.

Appeal to authority is an effective ploy in establishing a credible basis for almost any position you decide to adopt, especially if you mix it with a modicum of obvious truths. It makes a convincing brew.

A few precautionary notes:

1. Select persuaders that are meaningful to your listener as an individual or as a member of a group with whom you know he is closely associated. If you're trying to verbally seduce a member of the DAR you wouldn't cite reports of the NAACP.
2. The premise you start with, the "hooker," must have the semblance of truth, or at least a high degree of plausibility. A slight distortion may go unheeded, but make too obvious a slip and the game could be over.
3. The authority you offer must be a credible witness for your contention. To offer Richard Nixon, for example, as a paragon of intellectual honesty would be like citing Dick Gregory before a White Supremacy rally in Chattanooga.
4. Don't cite someone, or a group, that has an obvious interest in what you're espousing.

You can occasionally use the *lack* of authority, the reverse of ethos, as a manipulative factor, like the appeal of a marketing executive to his superior:

"I know every marketing authority you can name frowns on this approach to our problem. But even some experts can't see the trees for the woods. Ford researchers cleared the Edsel as a brilliant concept, over the no-go recommendations of a low-level marketing researcher. And the Xerox process was turned down by two large companies as impractical, in one instance over the strong objection of a newly hired subordinate. It simply proves that too much agreement—even by the top authorities—could show a lack of critical disagreement."

> Every man finds a sanction for his simplest claims and deeds, in decisions of his own mind, which he calls Truth and Holiness.
> ———————————————————— *Emerson*

A wonderous thing, this human craving for approval from "above," but even more wondrous is our dependence upon signs of such approval, or some kind of accreditation—any kind. Diplomas. Plaques. Certificates. Testimonials. Endorsements.

The next time you visit a law office, look along the walls for a framed certificate attesting to admission to practice before the United States Supreme Court, the nation's highest tribunal. Impressed? Forget it.

The hand-embossed certificate is no more a symbol of ability or professional standing than a Rotarian plaque or Elks membership pin. Any lawyer in practice for at least three years can secure it by mail; all he needs is the sponsorship of two attorneys licensed to practice in the Supreme Court and a $25 fee. No more. He can be a first-class rogue in his professional or personal life, with the ability of a nitwit, and still qualify.

"Only a tiny fraction of those admitted ever come to this court to practice," the admissions clerk of the Supreme Court is quoted as saying. "About 300 lawyers, out of the 180,000 certified to practice here, ever appear during a term. But how they prize that certificate! And the authority behind it; 'Admitted to practice before the United States Supreme Court.'"

Take a cue from legislators who are particularly adept in "piling it on," when about to make a speech in a legislative session. I have seen senators stagger into the Senate chamber looking like overnight campers under the weight of reports, files, and books, which they never once opened during the course of their long harangue.

I once looked at the bulging file of a state Senator in Albany, one of many he brought into the chamber in support of a bill to lift certain restrictions on gambling. It looked impressive with its clutter of photostats, newspaper clippings, and carbons, all of which related to the care of grape vineyards in the wine district of New York.

"What the hell has this to do with your bill?" I asked.

He grinned. "No more, no less, than some of the garbage you'll hear thrown against me. But it looks damn good when I spill it out over my desk during the debate."

An Arizona Congressman remarked to me on the similar tactic of a Southern legislator who staggers onto the floor with a load of books and reports whenever he speaks in support of a bill, "looking like someone starting on a safari. Two page boys help truck the stuff to his desk." Impressive to freshmen Congress-men—old hat, and an overworked gambit, to veteran legislators.

The sheer bulk and tonnage of proffered authority is a powerful tool in any deceptive maneuver, frightening opposition or cowing it into submission. So take a page from the book of legislators: whatever it is you're trying to make credible, or whomever you want to impress, you'll be ahead with solid physical evidence that *presumably* proves you're right—the bigger and more authoritative the better. It's wise to make the top folder or report one that relates to what you're talking about, just in case.

Deception? To be sure, but no more than many other showcases of authority and approval, whether advertisements for cars, cigarettes, movies, or feminine hygiene. I recall an adver-tisement in a Los Angeles newspaper for a new play: "Outstand-ing . . . will leave an indelible impression." What the reviewer actually said was: "An outstanding example of pure trash. It leaves one with an indelible impression of sheer waste in talent, money, and time."

Authors too love symbols of "higher up," loading their trade books or technical manuals with extensive bibliographies and citations of revered authority. It shows deep research, with the author consulting every knowledgeable person since Moses and Aristotle. *A fortiori,* what he says must be true. So many authorities can't be wrong.

Unfortunately, most of this footnoting is born of a desire to impress, or a spuriousness badly in need of an infusion of ethos, even if concocted.

So, if you are preparing a term paper, or a technical book or manual—for example, a critical analysis of an industry trend—load it with references, even if their relevance is tenuous or debatable. The chances are remote that anyone will ever read them, much less evaluate them with a critical eye.

If you can't pinpoint an authority to give weight to what you're offering, try the "they" ploy, described earlier in this book.

"I discussed my idea with many business executives. *They* all like it, every one of them."

"I researched what the knowledgeable analysts say about the price of steel. *They* all say it's going up next year."

You don't need documentation, or a bill of particulars—

who said what, when, or where. "They" is an Olympian figure, amorphous and all-powerful. Repeat such a vague testimonial often enough and it acquires the ring of a Biblical pronouncement.

Simply take it for granted that the "ethos" is there, omnipresent, accredited beyond any reasonable doubt.

"It's been proven over and over."

"No one in a position to know, denies it. How could he? It's so obviously true."

"It's a fact known to every researcher, established beyond question."

No area can match religion in its reliance on "ethos" to establish the credibility of a person, or to compel belief in a specific creed or course of action. De Tocqueville, the French philosopher, observed in the mid-19th century:

"In arriving in the United States, the religious aspect of the country was the first thing that struck my attention . . . Religious insanity is very common in the United States."

I recall hearing a popular radio evangelist announce that he was holding in his hands the phone directories of the capital cities in four states. "Now I place them on this altar and offer a prayer for the healing of every man and woman listed there who is sick, sore or disabled. Yes, my friends," he intoned in pontifical solemnity, "every blessed one of them. *And they shall be healed.* Hallelujah! Pray with me."

This kind of lunacy is so pervasive it's impossible to describe the limitless deceptions that feed on it, in our social, business or political activities. So, if your maneuver can be married to some aspect of religious ethos, even if only marginally legitimate, you have an invaluable aid.

"God." "The Almighty," "Our Merciful Father." You don't dispute these accreditations, any more than you question Motherhood or the Brotherhood of Man.

You can also learn from the way lawyers use ethos to pay dividends in the courtrooms. Juries and judges are easily gulled by the "weight of solid authority." I have seen trial lawyers pile law books and bound transcripts in a mountainous heap on the counsel table, as if to proclaim to all: "See, this is what I have on my side."

Too often, it's part of the strategy of deception, a time-worn bluff that is beyond easy exposure. But this tactic is often "for real." Louis Nizer, for example, the well-know trial lawyer, manages to convey an unmistakable impression that he's researched his case down to the bare roots.

I have seen him place a large table in front of the jury, covered by volumes of typewritten testimony of the trial and the examinations before the trial. Depositions and exhibits are neatly lined up, all carefully indexed and marked for quick reference, and are referred to constantly during the trial. The tableau radiates authority, impeccably honest and precise.

"When you lift up and refer to volume after volume of exhibits, trial testimony and memoranda, you assert a degree of authoritativeness in what you say," he pointed out to a group of lawyers. "The jury senses that you are not relying on your recollection alone. Moreover, they will hear repeated parts of the testimony given days or weeks before. If a single juror recognizes part of what you relate, even a small part, he will be pleased with your honesty, as well as his memory. You have made him your partner, and increased many times over his confidence in your honesty."

But not all persuaders play the same game, although they may imitate the effort.

The play for ethos weighs heavy as a form of skullduggery during the course of a criminal trial. Picture this tableau:

Defense counsel, anxious to establish a rapport between his white client and several blacks on the jury in a criminal trial in Washington, D.C., arranged for Joe Lewis, the heavyweight champion, then in his prime, to enter the courtroom and sit near the counsel table. As soon as the court declared a recess and before the jury filed out, Lewis walked to the client, shook hands, put an arm around his shoulder, and carried on an animated conversation. It was an effective ploy, with a megaton effect on the jury, strong enough to win an acquittal.

No less effective was the tactic of defense counsel in the

Florida trial of a policeman on a charge of felonious assault.

"Your Honor." he announced near the close of his case, "at this time I would like to call my last witness."

Into the courtroom strode the quarterback of the Miami Dolphins, who testified to the good moral character of the defendant. Certainly an accused who knew Florida's Number One in sports and was certified by him as being of good character was incapable of committing the crime charged. There was no question after that as to the verdict.

I represented a white client accused of defrauding a number of black investors in a sales promotion. Our defense— lack of intent to defraud—was admittedly weak and needed an infusion of credibility. That it got, in good measure, from a half-dozen matronly black women hired to sit in the front row and engage the defendant in animated conversation at each recess, before adjournment and before the jury filed out. They unmistakably identified with the defendant.

To emphasize this to the four blacks on the jury, I announced to the court at the conclusion of my proof: "To save time, your Honor, I will forego using the character witnesses I had planned to put on the witness stand. The defense rests."

An acquittal followed. Improper? Cheap theatrics? No doubt about it. And I received a deserved rebuke from this court. But before you pass judgment, consider the nature of a criminal trial. It is not a search for the truth. It is basically a contest, with deception and bluff playing a major role. Justice stands blindfolded on the sidelines, a majestic irrelevance.

So let's be no less realistic about your business and professional dealings. The score may be keyed to complete honesty and openness, but what comes out is often quite different. Examine each situation for whatever ethos you can summon to your aid, even if marginal or illusory. It's not only a definite aid in the competitive world in which we move, but mandatory if you hope to compete on equal terms.

We may all be created equal, but unfortunately, as George Orwell pointed out, some are more equal than others.

14. Word Fog, Half Truths, No Truths, and Miscellaneous Deceptions

. . . in some fields, the bad fades into the good by such insensible degrees that the two are not capable of being readily distinguished and separated in terms of legislation.

——————————————— *Belle Terre v. Borass* 416 U.S. 1

The truth is so precious that it must sometimes be protected by a bodyguard of lies.

——————————————— *Winston Churchill (on wartime propaganda)*

Word Fogging

> Gratiano speaks an infinite deal of nothing . . . His
> reasons are as two grains of wheat hid in two bushels of
> chaff; you shall seek all day ere you find them, and when
> you have them, they are not worth the search.[1]
> ———————————————————— *Shakespeare*

Word fogging is an integral part of the dialogue in business,
professional, or political dealings. To master the art of word-
noise or doublespeak is no great feat; it requires no more than a
modicum of brain power to accomplish its aim.

What aim, you may ask if you are not too familiar with this
tool of deception. What do you hope to gain by fogging what
you want to express under a cloud of words, some intelligible,
others as clear as Sanskrit prose? The first reply that comes to
mind is "non-accountability," an easy (if transient) escape from
what logically or legally is your own responsibility. Less obvious,
the masking of an intention, not entirely legitimate or to the
advantage of another.

But the most common use of word-noise—and one that
entrepreneurs and statesmen have honed to perfection—is observed in those situations where a person simply makes a pronouncement, and finds it expedient to conceal that actually he has
nothing to say. So he talks without communicating. Mincing your
words makes it a lot easier if you later have to eat them.

Word-fogging is a natural attribute of the corporate or
government spokesman. "I have been misquoted" usually means
"I wish to hell I never said it," just as "frank and full discussion"
denotes total disagreement, with no accord in sight. No less tricky
is the word clouding found in the annual reports of so many
corporations, concealing more than they reveal, confusing what is
best left unexplained.

> No one means all he says, and yet very few say all they
> mean, for words are slippery and thought is viscous.
> ———————————————————— *The Education of Henry Adams*

Not all word-fog is a put-on. To some, oral diarrhea is a natural
attribute. Hubert Humphrey, with his Gatling-gun pace, was an

example of exuberance spilling over in a torrent of words. A calculated delivery, words weighed carefully, would be as unnatural to Hubert as it would to Bob Hope. His speeches were, in the words of one wit, "a chaos of clear ideas."

But not all gushers have the moral restraints of a Humphrey, who exhausted more people than he persuaded. Some use the avalanche maneuver to divert your attention from a point you are trying to make, or dilute its impact, burying, clouding, or twisting it beyond recognition; others hope sheer volume will impress the listener, or perhaps enhance their own credibility, which it often does. Certainly nobody who spoke as fast as Hubert could be a calculating man.

Trial lawyers are only too familiar with the loquacious, unstoppable witness who spouts hearsay testimony in a gush of words, using a torrent where only a handful would do, squirming and sliding out from under the persistent questioning of the examiner. Getting a direct reply is like trying to nail a glob of Jell-O to a tree.

Where an accurate description, in conventional terms, ties you in too tight, try blunting it with word fog, like the aviation official who described a plane crash into a hillside as "a controlled flight into terrain." And you don't call miscalculations in your job "mistakes." This immediately raises questions of your competency. They are "an unanticipated result," "shortfall," "the effects of many variable factors," "a temporary setback," or a "non-recurring situation."

Never use the unvarnished truth in your criticism, if it may later haunt you. An educator, critical of a conference drowning in a sea of words, warned the participants of being "over-consensused," a polite way of describing oral garbage or plain horseshit. As informative as a caution by a legislator to a group of government planners to avoid "utopianizing."[2]

Doctors know instinctively how to hide bad news in a word cloud.

"Well, doctor, what do you think? What are my chances?"

"You never can tell. They're discovering new remedies every day."

"OK, but my chances?"

"Like I said—"

"Please, doc, the chances."

"Chances! Chances! You don't talk that way about a sickness or disease. There are so many imponderables, things you can't begin to guess at, etc. etc."

Word-fogging is actually a diversionary ploy. You're switching attention by changing the bait. Roosevelt, a master in the devious, tried unsuccessfully in 1940 to give England a large loan to buy war material. Congress shuddered at the cost involved. The President decided on a new tack. He called a press conference and explained he was dropping the dollar sign for a more humane approach.

"Suppose my neighbor's house catches fire and I have a long garden hose. . . ."

The idea caught on. The fire simply had to be doused. No question about it. It could burn our own ass. And so the course of history was changed.

While each player will have his own rules, depending on his native ingenuity and his instinctive appraisal of the other, there are a few common gambits you should be aware of. I am not advocating your conscious use of them as a tool of deception (most likely you've been using them regularly in your everyday activities), but only that you be forewarned in the event you find yourself a *nebbish* in the jungle of doublespeak.

"Please don't worry about it. Believe me, it's under control." Start worrying; you can smell the defensiveness.

"What the hell are you concerned about? You're my friend. And I don't go around screwing my friends." Your shafting is not far off.

"Stay put. I'll let you know if anything develops." Forget it. The message is clear: "Don't call me. I'll call you."

"You can check my standing with any of the banks in town." Try doing just that. You may be surprised.

None of us could live with an habitual truth teller, and thank goodness, none of us has to. An habitual truth teller is simply an impossible creature; he does not exist, he never has existed. Of course there are people who *think* they never lie, but it is not so—and this ignorance is one of the very things that shame our so-called civilization.

——————————————————— *Mark Twain*

If concealment is your objective, and word-fogging, half-truths, or no-truths are your weapons, there are a few precautions to be observed. Your intent must be hidden from view—not partially, but completely—and your message framed in plausibility.

Facts that you would prefer remain hidden should either be ignored (unless their omission would be too obvious) or so mixed with half-truths as to be unrecognizable. If your word-fog is carefully planned, detection is unlikely.

For example, a few years ago I instituted suit against a large drug manufacturer for marketing a drug (Mer 29) that caused a wide range of serious side effects. Results of initial testing reflected these effects, but were concealed in a clever mix of word cloud and half truths, with no credible warning to users. All damage suits were settled before trial, with the company pleading guilty in a criminal prosecution. Several million dollars was paid out in settlement of the suits.

What is remarkable is the ingenious smoke screen of words and phrases concocted by the defendant to hide the results of its testing procedures. I used the word "credible" above, because buried in the matrix of their literature were intimations of the truth. But the word-fog was so thick, you were hard put to find it.

An isolated case? Far from it. The medical director of another company, E. R. Squibb & Sons, resigned in 1957, because he reached a point "where I could no longer live with myself." He pointed out that a drug company doctor "must learn to word a warning statement so it will appear as an *inducement* to use the drug, rather than a warning of the dangers inherent in its use."[3]

An isolated industry? Hardly. Look at your automobile or household insurance policies, or the warranties on your appliances. Most are sprinkled with escape clauses, as readable as Einstein's theory of relativity.

You don't have to reach these skills in the report, summary, or lecture you're preparing. If there are matters you would prefer to gloss over or hide, you'll find you need only average ability to carry out the suggestions I made earlier. Believe me, they work. I've used them as a lawyer for over forty years. You'll find, too, that the person most critical of these maneuvers is usually the one most skilled in their use.

The Half Truth

> Add a few drops of deception to a half truth and you have an
> absolute truth.

To tell an untruth is not always to tell a lie. There is a basic
difference between lying and faking. Arthur Herzog, in his 1973
book *The B.S. Factor,* explained the difference. A lie is a statement
susceptible of immediate disproof. Something palpable. Like
saying you're six foot seven when you measure only five-two.
Something you can easily get caught at. Only children and idiots
commit this sin.

Herzog notes that America will probably be the first civilization to eliminate lies and give fakery its proper place in society.
To fake is simply to create an impenetrable mix of truths and half
truths.

Look around you. In pronouncements by government
spokesmen, business executives, lawyers, and judges, and even in
conversations with your business associates or mate, you'll see
fakery falling like mist in a London fog. Now suppose you suspect
that what you are about to offer may not be entirely acceptable in
the form presented. Draw a lesson from the flood of fakery in
which you move: add an infusion of half truths and untruths. It's
simple. Natural. "Something like snoring. You can do it in your
sleep."

> Sin has many tools, but a half truth is a handle
> that fits them all.

The listener's translation of what you say may not be precisely
what you intended. But only a dimwit will half-truth or fog it to
the point of non-recognition. Translations, however, present certain hazards—like a recent incident in the United Nations As-
sembly, when a delegate used in his speech the phrase, "out of
sight, out of mind." A Russian translator rendered it "Blind and
therefore insane."[4]

The amenities of everyday living allow for a wide variety of
these manipulations. You can't avoid them. So polish them.

Would you tell a plant manager his report is pure b.s. when you know how long he labored over it? Or the applicant for your secretary's job that the answer is "No. Definitely no. You're too damn homely?" Mark Twain put it neatly when he said "An injurious lie is an uncommendable thing; and so, also, and in the same degree, is an injurious truth—a fact which is recognized by the law of libel."[5]

A half truth is often indistinguishable from the whole truth. For example, a gateman testified in an action involving a collision between a train and an automobile. The cross-examiner hammered hard at his insistence that he stood at the crossing, swinging a lantern, as the train approached. The jury believed the gateman and nonsuited the plaintiff. A spectator later remarked: "You never did say if that lantern was lit."

The gateman chuckled: "I wasn't asked."

Lawyers use the half truth instinctively. To defense counsel, it is never "the theory of our case" but "the facts, the hard facts that we will prove to you."

So, if the entire scenario of what you are offering, whether a product, a service, or a cause you are espousing, renders it unpalatable, look for a few scraps of half truths. There is a simplistic beauty in this tactic, particularly when you know your deception is barely recognizable. Rare is the manipulator where diligent search won't uncover a particle of truth you can use, a glittering miscrocosm that you can color to your advantage.

Squeamish about using this maneuver? Don't be. It abounds on all sides. Consider, for example, the full page advertisement of a large motor company: "The vegetation in your backyard gives off as many hydrocarbons as the law permits in your car." *Ergo:* the furor over auto pollution is a tempest in a teapot.

True, vegetable emissions equal auto emissions. Omitted is the fact that the latter include carcinogens implicated as a cause of human cancer. The former is harmless. To imply they are the same is an example of a half truth. How many saw through the deception?

In the event you are selling or promoting a manufactured product, you can take a lesson from so many of our national advertisers. It's a simple deception, one you can easily apply.

Simply *add an ingredient not already present in your competitor's product.*

It can be totally irrelated to quality or performance, and have nothing to do with the natural mix of what you're selling, so long as you get an opinion from a laboratory or technician in the field that the new ingredient *may,* in some manner, add to performance, even in miniscule amount.

These opinions are not too difficult to secure. Long experience in the trial of product liability cases has repeatedly demonstrated that for a proper fee, you will (if you try long enough) find an accredited authority to certify what you want certified, short of asserting a patent untruth, like cyanide adding to the wholesomeness of your favorite bread or cake mix. This will serve to satisfy the truth-in-advertising code, more honored in the breach than observance. For example:

"The only plant food containing natural protein." What if protein adds nothing to plant growth?

Deception? Yes, of the first dimension. Lie? No. What you are saying is an absolute truth—no less than describing Retsyn as "the precious ingredient in Certs. No other mouth freshener has it." True. Now, what is Retsyn? A vegetable oil. The effect on bacteria in the mouth, or mouth odor, is the same as rinsing with Mazola.

These claims tell the truth—it's just that they don't tell the *whole truth.* It's somewhat akin to the Oregon pear grower who found his crop badly pitted following a hailstorm. The appearance of the pears made it unlikely his mail order customers would buy his product. A suggestion by his advertising man served to sell out the entire crop. The advertisements and mailing literature simply stated: "The *only* genuine pitted Oregon pears. Flavor unsurpassed. Accept no substitute."

The moral is clear. If you're hard put to come up with an arresting gimmick for your product or service, fall back on the *"More than,"* or *"the only one with"* claim. It's a universal half truth.

I have come to the conclusion—reluctantly, believe me— that there is a curious sickness afoot in our society, in our eagerness to accept the partial truth for the whole truth, facsimiles for the original. A popular entertainer looks, sounds, and dresses like Elvis Presley. The audiences know he is not the real Elvis, but girls swoon when he performs and try to kiss his feet. There is a singing group that sounds and dresses like the Beatles. Audiences scream at each performance. and the women pretend the same enjoyment as when the original Beatles performed—fully aware of the half truths they are wallowing in.

The Abstraction   Now consider those beautiful abstractions. How alluring and seductive! How neatly they hide your perfidy while you make like Billy Graham!

Their deception quota is low; on a rating of 0 to 10, it would rate 1 or 2, and the chances of discovery of your manipulation not much higher. Abstractions offer a safe harbor, a fail-safe maneuver when specificity would expose your deviousness.

If, for example, the situation you are in raises serious questions of your culpability, look for an abstraction to separate you from responsibility. Lyndon Johnson hid his miscalculations behind "peace with honor," "moral commitments," the "domino theory." Impressive, but meaningless. For a time, the abstractions worked; then they lost credibility and ultimately led to his downfall.

"Permanent guest artist" is as deceptive as "nonviolent force." "Department of Defense" (actually Department of War; you don't declare a defense), "selective pacifism," or "genuine facsimile."

I confronted a strong apologist for the PLO movement, a teacher at one of our Southern universities, with the latest terrorist incursion into Israel. "There are no villains, actually," he replied. "It's the flow of history, the rise and fall of nations and peoples. Like tidal movements beyond control." He neatly disassociated himself from the criminality of the acts, the slaughter of women and children, even from the PLO. An effective maneuver, making unnecessary a defensive posture or long-winded exposition on the hapless refugees from Palestine. Everybody is guilty. Nobody is guilty. There is no single act to condemn or defend.

Praised be the abstraction! Its use is becoming increasingly common. Statistical summaries, such as nine out of ten do this or that, are no more than abstractions. They can serve a noble or ignoble purpose, depending on what it is you are trying to hide or minimize.

Our government poured billions into military aid for Pakistan, only to find that the West Pakistanis used the assistance to ravage an independence movement in East Pakistan, slaughtering over a million and ravaging the countryside. Our blunder was labeled "international security assistance" in the federal budget. It took Senator Proxmire to uncover what lay behind this abstraction.

Proven dangers from drugs are reported as "statistically significant," instead of potentially dangerous. A grant to an airline, as Pan-Am, of a hundred million to continue operations, is called subsidy, while an increase in assistance to the indigent is described as a "handout." Mexicans who sneak across the border are no longer illegal aliens, but "undocumented aliens."

Those Beautiful Isms   Be ever alert for an *ism* to cover a weakness in your major premise or give an air of profundity to what might otherwise pass for nonsense.

"My opponent supports monopoly capitalism. No doubt about it. Is that what you want?"

"Make no mistake about it. This measure is a giant step toward corporate fascism."

Obviously it would be stupid to give a bill of particulars on what you mean. Vagueness is your cover. Your listener will conjure his own vision. The *ism* can be a halo or a noose, depending on the context in which you use it and the note of censure or praise you sound.

Which leads to a final caveat. The wording of your abstraction is important. It must be totally devoid of any suggestion of deception or self-interest. The shifting of responsibility must be credible and point to no one—least of all to yourself.

Notes

Chapter 1   The Statistical Trap

1. *King Richard III*, Shakespeare
2. *The Figure Finaglers*, Robert Reichard. McGraw Hill, p. xi
3. *Practical Statistics*, Russel Langley. Drake Publishers
4. *Pythagoras* in 520 B.C.
5. *The Figure Finaglers*, ibid. p. 39
6. "Editorial" in *News-Sun*, Sun City, Arizona
7. *How To Lie With Statistics*, Darrell Huff. W. W. Norton, p. 40
8. *The Peter Plan*, Laurence J. Peter. Wm. Morrow Co. p. 21
9. New York *Daily News*, Jan. 30, 1978
10. *How To Lie With Statistics*, ibid. p. 128
11. *The New York Times*, Nov. 2, 1925
12. "Journal of American Statistics," 1949, p. 463
13. *How To Lie With Statistics*, ibid. p. 16
14. *National Enquirer*, February 28, 1978, p. 3
15. & 16. *Practical Statistics*, ibid. p. 13
17. *The Great Storyteller*, François Rabelais
18. & 19. *How To Lie With Statistics*, ibid. p. 48, p. 93
20. *The Figure Finaglers*, ibid. p. 46
21. *Guides to Straight Thinking*, Stuart Chase. Harper & Row, p. 101

Chapter 2   The Great Put-On

1. *The Passionate State of Mind*, Eric Hoffer. Harper & Row
2. *The Decay of the Art of Lying*, Mark Twain
3. *The Oracle, a Manual of the Art of Discretion*.
4. *Time* Magazine, September 4, 1972
5. *Twelfth Night*, Act II, Shakespeare
6. *Cyrano de Bergerac*, Edmond Rostand
7. *Inside Intuition*, Flora Davis. McGraw Hill.

Chapter 3   The Executive Masquerade

1. *1876—A Novel*, by Gore Vidal. Random House, Inc.
2. *The Human Zoo*, Desmond Morris. McGraw Hill
3. *The Merchant of Venice*, Shakespeare
4. & 5. *Heroes and Heroines of Fiction*. William Walsh. Lippincott
6. *Power*, Michael Korda. Random House, p. 61
7. *Collected Essays*, Ralph Waldo Emerson

Chapter 4   Lawyer Put-Ons

1. *Peer Gynt*, Henrik Ibsen
2. *Yankee Lawyer: The Autobiography of Ephraim Tutt*. Charles Scribner's Sons

Chapter 5   The Research Project

1. *Harpers* Magazine, Oct. 1978, p. 13
2. *National Enquirer,* March 14, 1978, p. 61
3. *Newsweek,* March 13, 1978, p. 27
4. *Miami Herald,* April 19, 1978, p. 10A
5. *National Enquirer,* March 14, 1978, p. 61

Chapter 6   The Diversionary Ploy

1. *The New York Times,* April 14, 1978, p. A27
2. *Yankee Lawyer, The Autobiography of Ephraim Tutt,* Charles Scribner's Sons
3. *Do You Solemnly Swear?* Lewis Heller. Doubleday & Co.
4. & 5. *The Great Mouthpiece,* Gene Fowler. Harper & Row
6. *Final Verdict,* Adela Rogers St. John. Doubleday & Co.

Chapter 8   Who—Not What

1. *The Wisdom of Laotse,* Modern Library. Random House, Inc.
2. & 3. *Guides to Straight Thinking,* Stuart Chase. Harper & Row p. 59

Chapter 9   Stroke Him, Man, Stroke Him

1. *Illusion in Nature and Art.* Charles Scribner's Sons
2. *King Richard III.* Shakespeare
3. *Touching.* Ashley Montagu. Harper & Row
4. *National Enquirer,* August 23, 1977, p. 16
5. *Inside Intuition.* Flora Davis. McGraw-Hill

Chapter 10   The Manipulated Response

1. *The Great Storyteller.* Francois Rabelais
2. *The Passionate State of Mind,* Eric Hoffer, Harper & Row

Chapter 11   That Beautiful Man of Straw

1. *The Decay of the Art of Lying.* Mark Twain
2. *King of the Courtroom.* Michael Dorman. Copyright © 1969 by Michael Dorman, Dell Publishing Co.

Chapter 12   The Illusion of Relevancy

1. *The Merchant of Venice.* Shakespeare
2. *All for Love.* John Dryden
3. & 4. *Guides to Straight Thinking.* Stuart Chase. Harper & Row, p. 81
5. *The Rubáiyát of Omar Khayyám.* Edward Fitzgerald

Chapter 14   Word-Fog, Half Truths, No Truths, and Miscellaneous Deceptions

1. *The Merchant of Venice.* Shakespeare
2. *Wall Street Journal,* Feb. 9, 1978. editorial page
3. *Power, Inc.* Morton Mintz and Jerry S. Cohen, Viking Press p. 317
4. *New York* Magazine, April 3, 1978, p. 9
5. *The Decay of the Art of Lying.* Mark Twain